D0623472

HILLSBORO PUBLIC LIBRARIES
Hillsboro, OR
Member of Washington County
COOPERATIVE LIBRARY SERVICES

HAND

DECORATING

PAPER

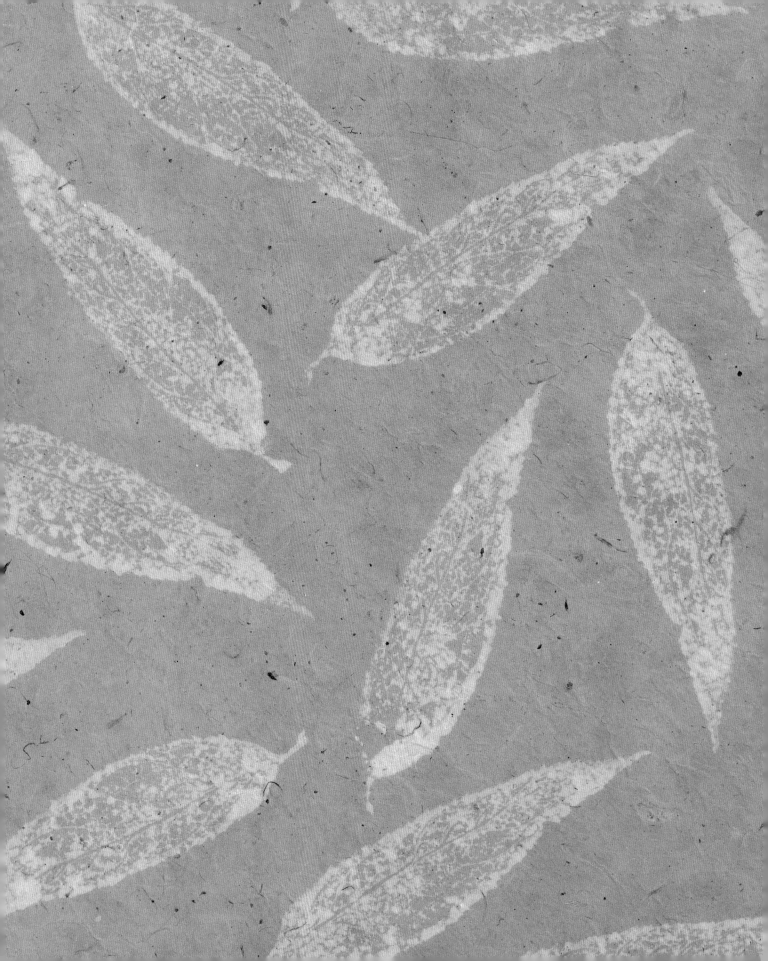

HAND

DECORATING

PAPER

MARIE BROWNING

Sterling Publishing Co., Inc.

New York

HILLSBORO PUBLIC LIBRARIES
Hillsboro, OR
Member of Washington County
COOPERATIVE LIBRARY SERVICES

Prolific Impressions Production Staff:

Editor: Mickey Baskett
Copy and styling: Laney Crisp McClure
Graphics: Lampe-Farley Communications, Inc.
Photography: Jerry Mucklow
Administration: Jim Baskett

Every effort has been made to insure that the information presented is accurate. Since we have no control over physical conditions, individual skills, or chosen tools and products, the publisher disclaims any liability for injuries, losses, untoward results, or any other damages which may result from the use of the information in this book. Thoroughly read the instructions for all products used to complete the projects in this book, paying particular attention to all cautions and warnings shown for that product to ensure their proper and safe use.

No part of this book may be reproduced for commercial purposes in any form without permission by the copyright holder. The written instructions and design patterns in this book are intended for the personal use of the reader and may be reproduced for that purpose only.

Library of Congress Cataloging-in-Publication Data Available

Published by Sterling Publishing Company, Inc.
387 Park Avenue South, New York, N.Y. 10016

Produced by Prolific Impressions, Inc.
160 South Candler St., Decatur, GA 30030
©2000 by Prolific Impressions, Inc.

3026 9863   4/04

Distributed in Canada by Sterling Publishing
c/o Canadian Manda Group, One Atlantic Avenue, Suite 105
Toronto, Ontario, Canada M6K 3E7
Distributed in Great Britain and Europe by Cassell PLC
Wellington House, 125 Strand, London WC2R 0BB, England
Distributed in Australia by Capricorn Link (Australia) Pty. Ltd.
P.O. Box 6651, Baulkham Hills, Business Centre, NSW 2153 Australia

Printed in China
All rights reserved
Sterling ISBN 0-8069-2753-4

About the Author

Marie Browning is a consummate craft designer, making a career of designing products, writing books and articles, plus teaching and demonstrating. You may have already been charmed by her creative designs and not even been aware; as she has designed stencils, stamps, transfers, and a variety of other products for national art & craft supply companies.

You may also have enjoyed books and articles by Marie. She is the author of four other books published by Sterling, *Beautiful Handmade Natural Soaps* (1998), *Handcrafted Journals, Albums, Scrapbooks, & More* (1999), *Making Glorious Gifts from the Garden* (1999) and *Memory Gifts* (2000). Her articles and designs have appeared in *Handcraft Illustrated*, *Better Homes & Gardens*, *Canadian Stamper*, *Great American Crafts*, *All American Crafts*, and in numerous project books published by Plaid Enterprises, Inc.

Browning earned a Fine Arts Diploma from Camosun College and attended the University of Victoria. She is a Certified Professional Demonstrator, a professional affiliate of the Canadian Craft and Hobby Association, and a member of the Stencil Artisan's League and the Society of Craft Designers.

Marie Browning lives, gardens, and crafts on Vancouver Island in Canada. She and her husband Scott have three children: Katelyn, Lena, and Jonathan.

Acknowledgements

Marie Browning wishes to thank the following manufacturers for their generous contributions of materials used in this book:

CTI Paper USA, Inc.
Sun Prairie, WI
for Kromecoat papers

Plaid Enterprises, Inc.
Norcross, GA 30092
www.plaidonline.com
For FolkArt® Acrylic Colors, acrylic varnishes, Decorator Blocks™, Decorator Block Glazes, and Combing Tools.

Environmental Technology, Inc.
Fields Landing, CA
www.eti-usa.com
For two-part, pour on resin

Delta Technical Coatings, Inc.
Whittier, CA
www.deltacrafts.com
For Ceramcoat acrylic paints, Paper Paints, fabric dyes and Marble Thix

Co-Motion Rubber Stamps, Inc.
Tucson, AZ 85706
www.comotion.com
For heat-sensitive foam blocks such as Dyna Blocks or PenScore.

Ranger Industries, Inc
Tinton Falls, NJ
www.rangerink.com
For Nature Printing Kit

Personal Stamp Exchange
Santa Rosa, CA
www.psxstamps.com
For rubber stamps and accessories

Speedball Art Products Co.
Statesville, NC
For pigmented acrylic inks, waterproof transparent inks, water soluble block printing inks, brayers and speedy cut blocks

Buckingham Stencils
Vancouver, BC Canada
www.buckinghamstencils.com
For stencils and roller stencil equipment

Boutique Trims, Inc.
South Lyon, MI
A large selection of decorative charms in many finishes.

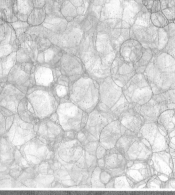

Table of Contents

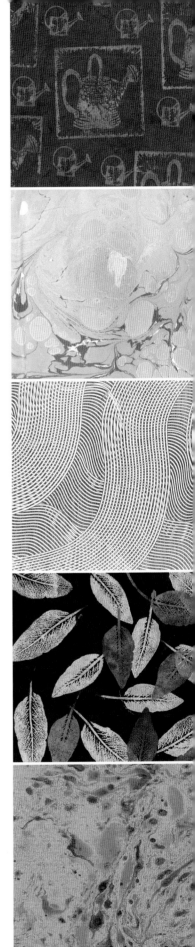

A Guide to Making Beautiful Decorative Papers with Simple, Easy to Find Materials

Making your own decorative papers for your crafting and packaging is rewarding and materials and equipment are generally inexpensive. Artistic skills are not required and any mistakes made are easily looked upon as an interesting aesthetic alternative! This book will display many different techniques in making beautiful papers and the simple instructions will guide you through a wide variety of historic and modern creative effects. The techniques discussed in this book range from simple to advanced, so you are sure to find something that will fit your skill level and tap into your creativity.

Some of the techniques included are paste paper, tie-dye paper, and printed papers, as well as, stamped, stenciled and marbled papers. After creating your decorative papers, you can use them in card designs, collage work, coverings, bookbinding, memory albums, packaging and general crafting projects.

Papers have been decorated by hand for centuries. We can recreate some of the traditional treatments with simple tools and materials that are readily available. The decorative papers available for purchase are varied and beautiful, but the papers that you can create with your own imagination are more rewarding and much less expensive. Do not hesitate to combine these techniques for even more varied papers. For example, combine splattering on a stenciled piece, or try salting and the tie-dye method together. The possibilities are endless! 🖐

Supplies for Paper Decorating

Paper

Choosing the right paper is an important factor when deciding on your decorative technique. Some methods are only suited to specific types of paper. The individual technique instructions will list the types of papers that are best suited for that particular technique.

The **weight and texture** of the paper is an important factor to consider so that you will achieve the effect you wish with the technique you have chosen. Heavy 400lb watercolor paper may not wrinkle when paint is applied, but it is far too thick to use to bind a book. Lighter weights of paper are generally better for decorative purposes, as they are easier to work with. The techniques in this book describe methods of keeping the paper from wrinkling while working on it. The texture, whether smooth and hot pressed or a rough, handmade rag paper, is an important element when choosing your paper. Smooth, shiny commercial printing coated paper is perfect for some methods such as bubble paper and paste paper, but unsuitable for seaweed marbling and tie-dye paper.

Other qualities to consider when choosing paper are the absorbency rate, strength and the color. For example, you will want a paper that quickly absorbs moisture for the tie-dye method, but you may not want an absorbent paper when stenciling.

Types of Papers to Use

White Copy Paper: For most of the techniques, white copy paper or bond paper (the type that is used in photocopy machines) can be used and is readily available everywhere. The large 11" x 17" is a good size so that you will have enough for a project.

Cartridge Paper: You can also find large rolls of cartridge paper (used in some photocopy machines) in stationery outlets. These rolls make it easy for you to cut off the size you need. These rolls are perfect to use for creating wrapping paper or to use for large projects.

Watercolor Paper: This is a very absorbent paper and works well with waterbased paints. It comes in various weights and textures. Be sure to consider the weight as it relates to the project for which you are going to use the paper.

Coated Papers: You can find many coated papers in print shops. There are a wide variety of commercial print coated papers that can be used for paper decorating. They are shiny and non-absorbent. This allows the paint to be "moved around" on the surface. A brand of commercial printing coated paper you may find available is Kromecoat®. Less expensive coated papers that can be used are finger paint paper or freezer paper. Freezer paper is usually a plastic-coated white shiny paper.

Artist Drawing Papers: These are usually strong papers that take paint and ink nicely. They can be found in shops that carry art materials.

Japanese Rice Paper: This type of paper is thin, soft, and absorbent. It has no sizing or coatings. It works great for techniques in which you wish the paint or ink to be absorbed into the paper immediately.

Brown Paper: This is a great all purpose paper. It is strong, has a nice smooth surface, usually of a nice medium weight, and is not too absorbent. It can be found on rolls so that it is great for creating wrapping paper.

Art Papers: There is such a wide variety in this category that a generalization is not possible. Most art supply stores have a nice selection that will give your creativity a jump start.

Paints & Inks

The choice of paints or inks for each technique depends on the application. The best choice for each technique is given in the individual technique instructions, but in many cases, there is a list of alternatives that will work. Generally, acrylic craft paint is a good paint because it can be watered down to an inky consistency and used to color pastes or be mixed with a medium for printing. Some of the techniques require artist inks or tube oil paints for the best results. All of these paint mediums can be purchased in craft stores, art supply stores and stationery outlets.

Tools & Equipment

Generally, most of the tools and equipment needed are household items or can be easily found at local discount, craft or art stores. Challenge your creativity to find new uses for common tools and products. Even a simple kitchen tool such as a potato masher can create a striking pattern in the wet compound while creating a paste paper. More elaborate tools such as a block cutter, brayer or rubber combs can be found at most art supply or craft shops. Individual technique instructions give a complete list of the tools and equipment needed.

Your Workspace

I like to use a hard piece of plastic, about 1/8" - 1/4" thick, such as Plexiglas®, as a work surface. This will protect your tabletop and give you a stable surface on which to work. Many times I will cover this with freezer paper to absorb any paint, water, or other liquid. The freezer paper can then be thrown away and you won't have to clean your work surface. 🖐

Design Elements

Pattern

When designing your papers, making patterns is an important element for attractive, successful projects. Many patterns, such as a repeated diamond to create a harlequin design or alternate squares for a checkerboard design are the most uncomplicated yet the most striking patterns. A single leaf can be repeated to make an interesting pattern or used alone as fine, abstract art. Whereas the pattern in the paste paper shows the rhythm of the application, ink marbling shows the movement of the water frozen into the paper as a lovely, fluid pattern. Don't be shy in experimenting with your patterns and in repeating simple shapes to create unique and gorgeous papers.

Color

Color is a very important consideration when creating your papers. The best designs are a combination of only a few colors rather than many. Listed below is a simple color theory to help you identify colors and create new colors by mixing. A color wheel, found at art supply stores, can be helpful in choosing colors that work well together.

Basic Color Groups

Primary colors: Blue, red and yellow are the three basic primary colors and can be mixed to create any hue.
Secondary colors: These colors are created by mixing two primary colors together. For example, red + blue = purple, red + yellow = orange, and yellow + blue = green.
Tertiary colors: These colors are created by mixing primary colors with secondary colors. They produce colors such as yellow-green, blue-violet and red-orange.

Color Components

- Complimentary colors are colors that are opposite each other on the color wheel. The compliments of the primary and secondary colors are red and green, yellow and purple, and orange and blue.
- Shades are black and white, and when added to colors they create different tones such as light leaf green and dark hunter green.
- Color intensity indicates how bright or pure it is. To dull or mute a color, add its complimentary color.

What does all this mean? Well, for example, to mix a Dusty Rose you would first add red to white to create a pink tone. Then to mute it, add a tiny touch of its complimentary color, which is green. A French Blue is created by adding blue to white to create a medium light blue, then a touch of orange to mute it and create a beautiful soft blue. A few mixing points: Always add the darker color to the lighter color and always mix enough paint for the entire project. Experimenting with color mixing allows you to create many additional colors while only purchasing the primary colors of red, yellow and blue, and the shades of black and white. 🖐

Antiqued Paper

To achieve an antiqued or aged look to your paper, simply use tea or coffee to stain the paper and give it an ancient patina.

Supplies You Will Need

Paint

Prepared tea or coffee: The color in this technique comes from the tea or coffee. Whereas tea gives a brighter sepia tone, coffee has a soft, ivory hue.

Paper

Any absorbent paper is suitable for this technique.

Sponge

A nice marine sponge is best. Used to apply tea or coffee to the paper.

Decorating the Paper

1. Prepare tea by soaking a tea bag in a glass of hot water for about 8-10 minutes. If using coffee, brew as normal.
2. Sponge the strong tea or coffee solution onto the paper. Splashes and puddles are okay!
3. Sprinkle used coffee grounds onto the damp paper for a speckled effect, if desired. Let the paper dry flat.

Antiqued Paper Projects

Thank You Cards: Make cards by applying pieces of antiqued paper to the front of gift cards with a glue stick. Finishing is the addition of a torn piece of black art paper and a charm. Write a greeting below the charm with permanent ink pen.

Thank You Note: Make card by adhering a piece of antiqued paper to the front of a note card with a glue stick. Finishing is the addition of a bee charm. Write the words 'Thank you' with a permanent ink pen.

Batik Paper

The batik paper technique presented here uses a liquid masking fluid found in art supply stores instead of hot, melted wax, which is traditionally used for fabric batik. The masking fluid is painted, splattered, dabbed or dropped onto the paper, left to dry, and then the paper is washed with color. The masking fluid resists the paint and, when removed, leaves the masked areas unaffected. This method is easy to do and the results are dramatic.

Supplies You Will Need

Paint

Watercolors, gouache, drawing inks or acrylic paints are all good choices for this method. Thin the paints down to an inky consistency before using.

Paper

Paper with a smooth surface such as drawing paper, copy paper or lightweight watercolor papers are all acceptable for this method. Do not choose a paper with a soft, absorbent surface or the masking fluid may rip the paper when being removed.

Liquid Masking Fluid

This is for creating a resist pattern. This is a rubber-based liquid that is generally tinted blue or yellow so that it is easy to see on the paper. Shake well before using.

Other Tools & Materials

Paint brushes: for applying the masking fluid and paint. Use cheap glue brushes for the masking fluid, as it is not easy to wash out and can ruin good brushes. Plastic spray bottles with prepared paint can also be used to spray on the color.
White eraser: for removing the masking fluid.

continued page 16

Batik paper: masking fluid brushed on

Decorating the Paper

1. Apply the masking fluid to the paper surface. You can brush, sponge, stamp or splatter the fluid onto the paper. Let the masking fluid dry completely on the paper. It is best not to leave the masking fluid on the paper for long periods of time as it makes it more difficult to remove.

2. Wash paint onto paper with a brush or spray on with a spray bottle.

3. When the paint has dried, gently rub with your hand to remove the thin rubbery layer of mask. For stubborn patches, use a clean white eraser to rub off the mask. The masked images are clear and crisp.

Additional Batik Techniques

Experiment with multiple overlays of fluid and washes to build up your designs. Try printing the mask on with fresh leaves or using a calligraphy pen and nib to write on lettering with the masking fluid.

Batik Paper Projects

Gift Cards: Begin with a folded gift card. Attach a piece of batik paper to the front with glue stick. The paper in this example is stamped with masking fluid then washed with a brown-toned paint.

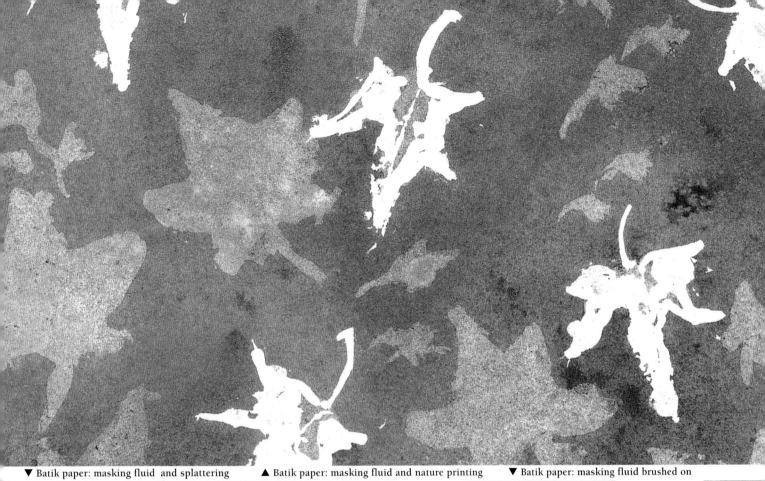

▼ Batik paper: masking fluid and splattering   ▲ Batik paper: masking fluid and nature printing   ▼ Batik paper: masking fluid brushed on

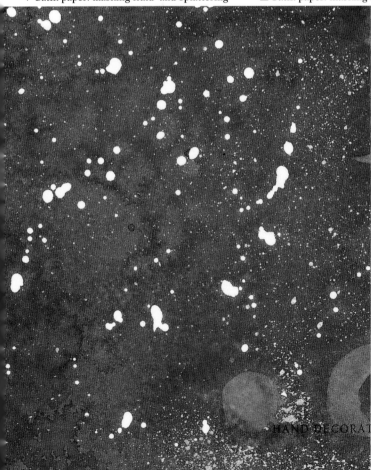

Batik Paper with Paint Resist

*This technique is a type of resist painting that uses readily found white acrylic paint.
It also is a wonderfully easy technique for creating an airy sky design on paper.*

Supplies You Will Need

Paint

White acrylic paint is used as the resist in this method. Unlike the masking fluid, the white paint is not removed from the paper after the design is applied. Use the white paint at full strength with no diluting. For adding color to your paper, use acrylic paints and thin them to a cream consistency before using. Apply the white acrylic paint with a sea sponge or a brush. Apply the colored acrylics with a large wash brush.

Paper

Paper with a smooth surface such as drawing paper, copy paper and lightweight watercolor papers are all acceptable for this method.

Tools & Materials

Sea sponges and brushes: for applying the white acrylic paint and the colored paint.
Spray bottle: for spraying on the prepared paints, if you choose.
Cellulose sponges: for removing excess paint. You can also use soft rags or paper towels.

continued page 20

Batik paper with paint resist, brushed.

Decorating the Paper

1. Brush or sponge the white paint onto the paper. Do not cover the entire paper with paint, as the design aspects come from the different look of the washed on color on both the paper and the paint surfaces. You can also manipulate the  white paint while still wet with a rubber comb or other tools to create texture. Let the white paint dry completely before proceeding.

2. When the white coat has dried, wash or spray on the thinned acrylic color.

3. Immediately after applying the color, wipe gently with a clean, damp sponge. The sponge will remove the excess paint from the white paint leaving color in the crevasses and dents in the paint. Wipe, if necessary, 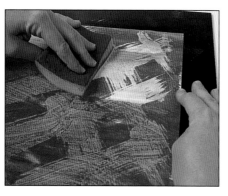 with a dry rag to accent the highlights. Add additional colors for added depth and interest.

Paint Resist Projects

Frame: Begin with a pre-purchased wooden frame. Attach paint resist paper to the frame with decoupage finish and a foam brush.

Pillow Box: Laminate a piece of paint resist paper to make it more sturdy. (See "Laminated Paper" for instructions on this technique.) Construct parcel using the pattern and instructions given in the section titled, "Making Envelopes & Boxes". Finish by attaching a rubber-stamped label to the front and a tie of sheer ribbon. 🖐

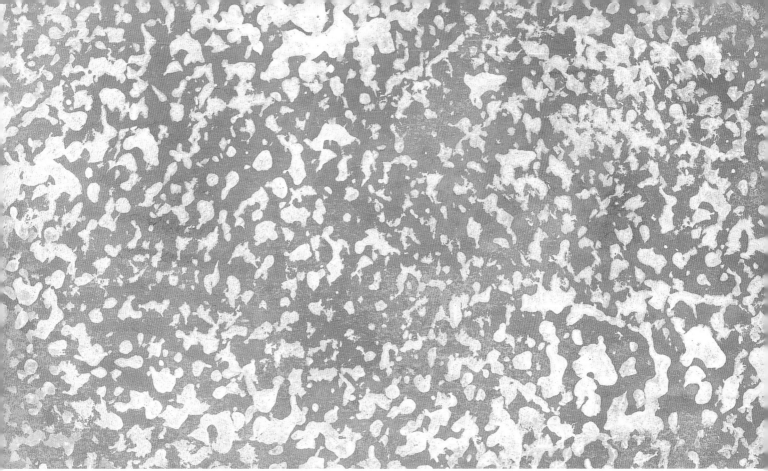

▲ Batik paper with paint resist, sponged on   ▼ Batik paper with paint resist, combed

Block Printed Paper with Purchased Blocks

Block printing is a classic technique that has been used for centuries to apply a design to paper. Carved wooden block printing in Japan has reached the height of quality and craftsmanship. Today, with the popularity of block printing as a technique for crafters to design and enhance their walls, there are a wide variety of pre-made blocks on the market. The designs are varied and reflect the latest trends.

Supplies You Will Need

Ink or Glaze

Water-based printing inks or acrylic glazes are the paints of choice for this method. Water-based printing inks make clean up far easier and the drying time of your decorative papers faster.

Paper

Smooth drawing paper, colored pastel paper, copy paper, absorbent rice paper and printing paper are all suitable choices for this technique.

Pre-purchased Blocks

There is a wide variety of types of blocks as well as designs. Today many blocks are made of a dense foam. Sometimes they will be called "stamps" — but do not confuse these with rubber stamps. You can purchase these from craft stores, home decorating stores and rubber stamp stores.

Other Tools and Materials

4" soft, rubber brayer: for rolling the paint onto the block. You can also use dense foam sponges to load the paint, but it takes more time.

Sheet of hard plastic or glass: for use as an inking plate. A 12" square piece is a good size. A large plastic plate that is flat and hard can also be used.

Palette knife: You can use a metal or a plastic one to spread the paint on the inking plate.

continued page 24

Block printed with purchased blocks and sponging ▶

Decorating the Paper

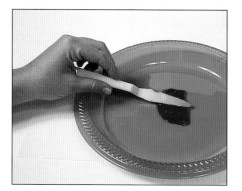

1. Squeeze the paint onto your inking plate and smooth out with a palette knife.

2. Roll the brayer over the paint, spreading it out evenly. Use paint immediately and do not let the paint dry on the inking plate. If you find the inking plate is drying out too quickly, cover with damp, not wet, paper towels between printings.

3. Roll the paint onto the block evenly making sure the entire surface is covered.

4. Press the block firmly onto the paper, pressing down evenly with your fingers, to produce a clean print.

5. Gently, lift the block from the paper to reveal the resulting print.

6. Repeat the inking and printing steps for more images. Add fresh paint to the inking plate as needed.

Block Printing Project

Round Box: Begin with a pre-purchased papier-mache box. Cover the box lid with paper that has been sponged and block printed. Paint the bottom of the box with acrylic craft paint and then sponge in metallic gold paint. When dry, coat the box with acrylic matte varnish. Finish with a gold ribbon and decorative fruit and leaves.

Block printed with purchased blocks and sponging ▶

Block Printed Paper with Cut-Your-Own Blocks

Cutting your own blocks opens up a wide array of possible patterns and images that can be used over and over again to create your own decorative papers and greeting cards.

Many materials can be used for the blocks. Traditional materials include linoleum, wood and even potatoes. White rubber erasers make excellent blocks that are easily cut and are now available in large size pieces especially for block printing. If you have ever cut into linoleum tile for creating decorative blocks, you will find this eraser-like material is much easier, faster and safer to carve. There are also commercial foam products on the market that can be used for the blocks. Block printing is fast and easy — you can cut detailed patterns into the blocks in a single afternoon and have finished printed cards by the evening. A bonus is that you can also cut into both sides of the block making it very economical to use.

Supplies You Will Need

Color

Water-based printing inks, rubber stamp pads with a raised pad or acrylic glazes can be used. Water-based printing inks make clean up far easier and the drying time of your decorative papers faster.

Paper

Smooth drawing papers, colored pastel papers, copy papers, absorbent rice papers and printing papers are all suitable choices for this technique.

Printing Blocks Supplies Shown Here

Linoleum tiles: Find the blocks in art supply stores and craft outlets.
Linoleum tile cutter and a variety of attachment tools: The cutters are available at art supply stores. You can also cut your design with an art knife, but you will be limited in the design as you will not be able to get the finer details.

Other Tools & Materials

Soft pencil: or graphite transfer paper for applying the pattern to the block.
Rubber stamp pad: with a raised pad. This is optional and is used for testing.
Rubber brayer: for applying the color to the block.

Sheet of hard plastic or glass: for use as an inking plate.

continued page 28

Block printed with cut-your-own blocks ▶

Making the Blocks

1. Draw a simple design on the block with a soft pencil. You can also use transfer paper to transfer a pattern from a copyright-free book or pattern book.

2. Cut the design into the block with the linoleum tile cutter. Go around the main motif with a straight blade, angling the cut away from the printed areas to make a strong block. Add the details with a small V-gouge cutter and cut away the non-printing areas with a larger U-gouge cutter. Do not cut too deeply, just enough to prevent the ink from seeping into the design. When you think you are finished, make a test print with the stamp pad. This will show you how the design will look and give you a chance to change or re-cut areas.

3. When you are satisfied with the design, brush off any loose bits and prepare your inking plate and papers to make decorative papers and cards.

Decorating the Paper

1. Apply color to the inking plate and smooth out with a palette knife. Push the brayer over the inking plate, spreading out the color evenly. Use paint immediately and do not let the paint dry on the inking plate. If you find the inking plate is drying out too quickly, cover with damp, not wet, paper towels between printings.

2. With the paint covered brayer. roll the color onto the block evenly making sure the entire surface is covered. If using a rubber stamp pad, ink the block until the surface is covered with an even coating of the color.

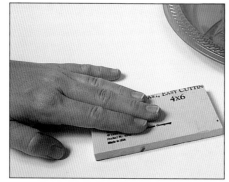

3. Press the block firmly onto the paper, pressing down evenly with your fingers, to produce a clean print. The block can be printed side by side or all over in a random pattern.

4. Gently, lift the block from the paper to reveal the resulting print. Repeat the inking and printing steps for more images. Add fresh paint to the inking plate as needed. Experiment with different colors and overlays of different patterns for an endless variety of patterns.

continued page 30

Cut-Your-Own Block Projects

Gift Cards: (see page 29) Begin with a folded gift card. Attach a piece of block printed paper to the front with glue stick. The papers in these examples are hand-cut blocks printed on black art paper with a pale gold metallic paint.

Wrapping Paper & Card: Begin with a roll of plain white paper, suitable for wrapping gifts. Use a hand-cut block and gold paint to fill the paper with the pattern. To make the card, repeat the stamp from one corner to another on the face of the card and write a message with a gold paint pen. After wrapping gift box with the paper, finish with sheer ribbons and a gold button.

Using Heat-Sensitive Foam Blocks

Available commercially is a foam block product that can be used for Cut-Your-Own Blocks. This product can also be used with a heating tool or other heated objects to create designs. This foam product allows versatility in making beautiful images from found images. The beauty of this product is that when you are finished with one image you can simply re-heat and press into a new texture. You will find this wonderful craft block in craft stores and rubber stamp outlets, distributed by several rubber stamp companies.

Decorating the Paper

1. Heat the surface of the foam block with the heat tool until soft. Immediately press into a texture. For example, experiment with pressing into a crack in the cement, a wire screen or a found metal ornament. You can also press into a pile of paper clips, a handful of rice or anything else around your home that will impart an interesting pattern.
2. Apply paint and print the same as you would other block printing techniques. 🖒

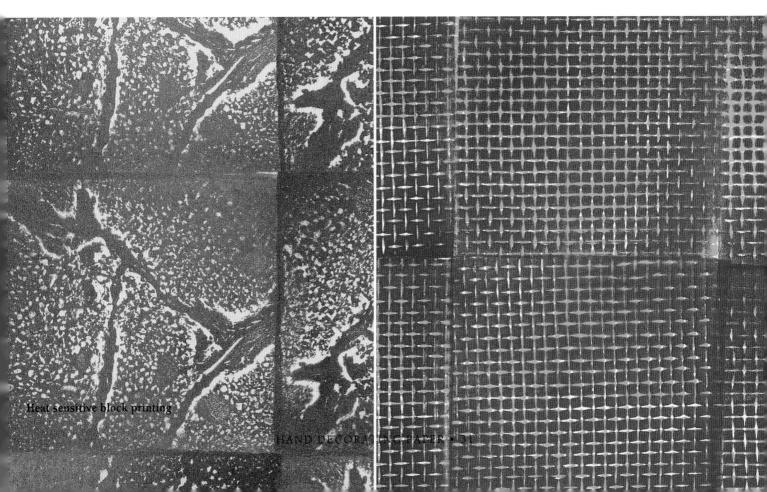

Heat sensitive block printing

Bubble Paper

This is a simple, fun and unusual form of decorative paper that can be produced by anyone. You would never guess that blowing bubbles could result in this intriguing design.

Supplies You Will Need

Inks

Use drawing inks prepared by thinning with water in a 1:1 ratio and adding a squirt of dishwashing liquid.

Paper

Shiny commercial printing coated paper works best with this method, but any paper with a smooth surface will work.

Other Tools & Materials

Plastic bowls: Use one for each ink color. Use disposable or recycled plastic containers for this technique.
Plastic straws: Use one for each ink color.
Clear dishwashing liquid: for making your inks bubble.

continued page 34

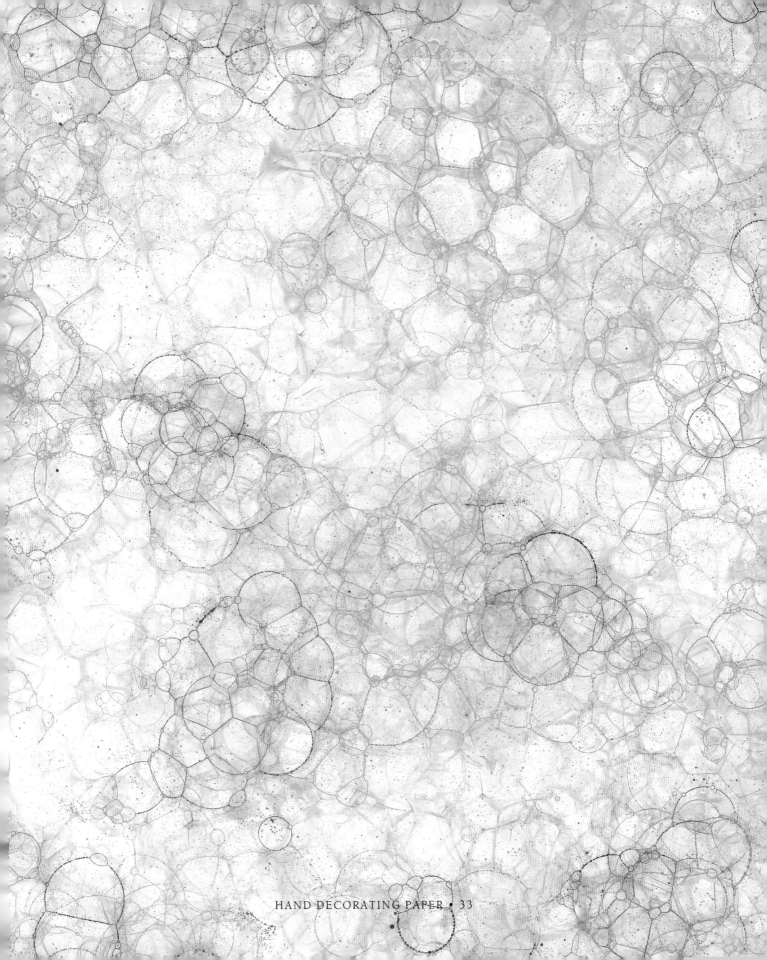

Decorating the Paper

1. Line up the plastic containers and fill them 1/3 full with the prepared ink colors. Place a straw for each color beside each bowl. Beginning with the first color, *gently* blow into the prepared solution filling the container with colored bubbles. Keep blowing until the bubbles have risen about 1" over the top of the bowl's rim.

2. Gently place the paper onto the bubbles, making a print.

3. Keep repeating this process with the additional colors until the sheet is covered with the bubble design. You will need to blow the bubbles into the colors each time you take a print. Let the bubbles that stick to the paper pop by themselves to create the clearest bubble images.

Bubble Paper Project

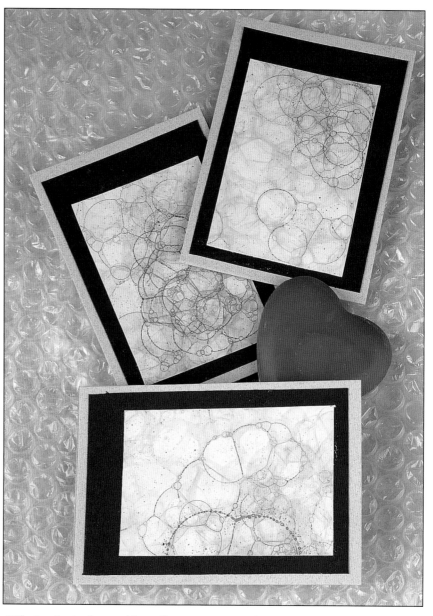

Gift Cards: Make card by adhering a piece of bubble paper to the front of a solid piece of art paper with glue stick. To finish, glue this to the front of a gift card. 🖐

Color Transfer with Tissue Paper

This technique produces a great colored paper that can be used as an interesting base for stenciled, stamped or printed images. It is inexpensive and requires no paints or inks as the color comes from the colored tissue paper. You not only produce multi-colored tissue, but also the white sheet of paper that the tissue sits on ends up with some fascinating colored patterns.

Supplies You Will Need

Color

The dye from the tissue paper yields the color for this project. The cheaper, multi-colored packages of tissue paper seem to be the best for this method.

Paper

The tissue paper is both the color and the finished decorative piece. You will also want to have a plain white paper as the base to create yet another piece of decorative paper. All types, from a smooth watercolor paper, plain copy paper or a shiny sheet of commercial printing coated paper will work with varying results. The sheet of white base paper and the tissue paper should all be cut to the same size. A good starting size is 9" x 12".

Tools & Materials

Spray bottle: filled with clean water.
Plastic gloves: for hand protection.

continued page 38

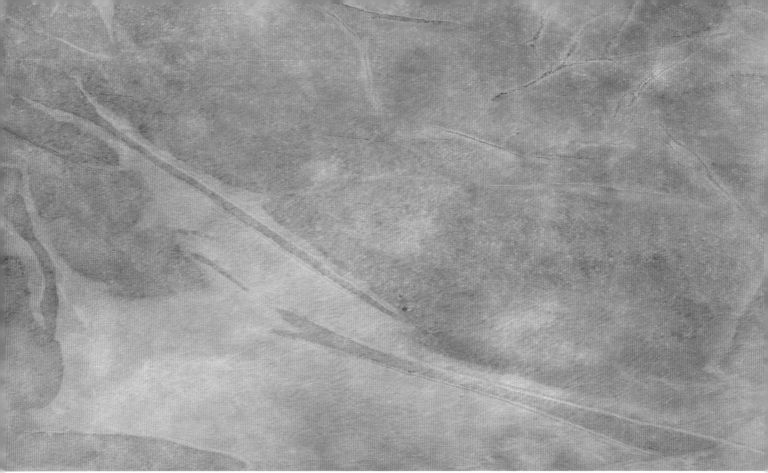

▲ Tissue paper laminated with freezer paper   ▼ Tissue paper laminated with freezer paper

Decorating the Paper

1. Place your sheet of white base paper on your workspace. Spray the surface well with the water.

2. Place a piece of colored tissue on top. Spray tissue paper with water again being careful not to spray so much as to make puddles.

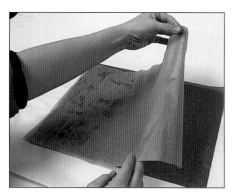

3. Place another sheet of colored tissue on top of the first.

4. Spray with water again. Repeat with different colors of tissue, spraying with water each time until you have a pile of about 6-8 sheets on top of each other.

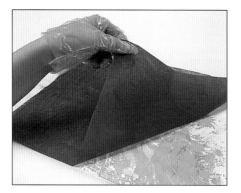

5. Let the pile sit and the dyes from the tissue sheets mingle and mix together. When the sheets are just damp, peel off the individual sheets and hang or lay flat to continue drying. The bottom white sheet will be beautifully colored with an interesting design as well. Even if the tissue paper looks a bit disappointing when wet, let it dry before judging your success, as the subtle patterns and colors are not entirely revealed until completely dry.

Additional Color Transfer with Tissue Paper Techniques

• To make the fragile tissue paper stronger and more usable, follow the instructions given for "Laminating Paper" given in the techniques section.

• Experiment with folding or scrunching the tissue paper before spraying and stacking for additional textures and patterns.

Color Transfer with Tissue Paper Project

Fleur De Lis Cards: Make cards by adhering pieces of color transfer paper to the fronts of gift cards. Finishing is a rubber stamped fleur de lis motif with metallic silver paint. 👑

Tissue paper — base paper

Tissue paper — base paper

Faux Leather Paper

Traditionally, leather was used extensively for bookbinding. With this method you can recreate the look of leather very inexpensively.

Supplies You Will Need

Paper

Tissue paper in tan, gold or brown color to use as the color for the faux leather look.

White or brown freezer paper to use as a base on which to laminate the tissue paper for strength.

Other Tools & Materials

Iron and ironing board: for pressing and fusing the papers.
Acrylic matte varnish: for sealing the paper.
Brush: for applying the varnish.

Decorating the Paper

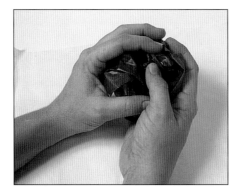

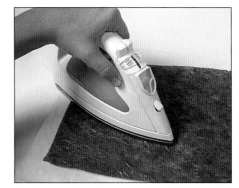

1. Crumple sheet of tissue paper tightly.
2. Carefully, smooth out the sheet of tissue. Place the freezer paper, shiny side up on ironing board. Place the tissue paper on top of the freezer paper. Fuse the papers together with the iron on high heat, no steam. The crinkles in the tissue will be flattened but will give the look of leather.

3. Brush on a topcoat of the matte varnish to strengthen and give the faux leather a realistic leather feel. If you choose a tissue color that suits your project, use as is. If you wish to antique or give some mottled shades to your faux leather, you can tint the acrylic varnish with a few drops of acrylic paint before applying.

continued page 41

Faux Leather Paper Project

Dragonfly Box: Begin with a pre-purchased cardboard or papier mache box. Cover lid and box with two different colors of faux leather papers. Cover bottom corners of box with paper from the lid. Use decoupage finish to attach paper to box. Attach a square of the paper used to cover the box onto the center of the lid. Finish by attaching a dragonfly charm with hot glue.

Faux leather

Laminated Paper

This is a technique for making delicate papers, like tissue and fine rice papers, sturdier and easier to use in book binding, as well as, covering and packaging projects.

Supplies You Will Need

Paper

Decorated paper to be laminated: Any delicate paper that you want to give more strength can be laminated. Techniques such as the Color Transfer from Tissue Paper and the Faux Leather work well with this laminating technique.

White or brown freezer paper to use as a base on which to laminate the tissue paper for strength.

Other Tools and Materials

Iron and ironing board: for pressing and fusing the papers.

Laminating the Paper

 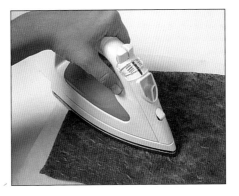

1. Iron the decorative paper until it is smooth.

2. Cut the freezer paper slightly smaller than your piece of decorative paper, and place it, shiny side up, on the ironing board. Place the decorative paper on top, making sure it covers

the freezer paper completely. Be sure your iron is on high and has no steam.

3. Press the papers together. The heat will melt the plastic coating on the freezer paper and fuse the papers together. Keep the iron moving to prevent scorching your paper. 🖐

Marbleized Paper with Ink

This is believed to be the oldest of all the paper marbleizing techniques. It is called sumingashi *and was developed in 12th century Japan. The inks are floated on a thickener/sizing and then printed onto absorbent papers.*

Supplies You Will Need

Inks

Quality drawing inks or Chinese inks work the best in this technique. Prepare the inks by mixing with water in a 1:1 ratio. You may need to add a few drops of rinsing agent to the inks if they are not dispersing onto the top of the water size.

Paper

An unsized, absorbent and strong paper is used for this technique. Lightweight printing paper, Japanese rice paper and good quality drawing paper are all good choices.

Other Tools and Materials

Large, flat container: like a 13" x 17" disposable tin foil roaster. Do not use a container that has already been used for the oil marbling technique because it will interfere with the process. Be sure that your pan is larger in size than your paper.
Water thickener for marbling: These thickeners are available from craft or art stores. If unable to locate, you can use the gelatin sizing used in the oil marbleizing technique or simply pour a bottle of liquid starch into the pan and use as is.
Old newspapers: roughly cut into 6" x 13" strips. These strips are used to skim the surface of excess ink after a print has been made and to prepare the bath for the next piece.

Plastic cups: or small plastic containers for mixing the ink.
Wooden craft sticks: for mixing the ink.
Photographic rinsing agent: (available at photo supply stores) for helping stubborn colors to disperse on the water surface and to create the ringed pattern.
Wooden skewers: for moving the ink around on the surface of the water.
Brushes: for dropping the ink onto the surface of the water. You will need a brush for each color and one for the rinsing agent if using it.

Sheet of hard plastic or glass: This should be at least 1" larger all around than your paper.
Workspace Tips: Organize your workspace close to a sink to rinse off the paper after the print has been made. Have everything close at hand for easy access. Have a large plastic garbage bag taped to the side of the table to dispose of the used newspaper strips.

continued page 46

Simple ink marbling

Decorating the Paper

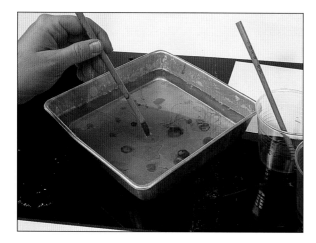

1. Prepare the water thickener according to the directions on the manufacturer's label. If using the gelatin sizing, follow the directions in the oil marbling section.

2. Drop the inks on the surface of the thickened water with a brush, just touching the surface with the tip of the brush to release the color.

3. Let the colors disperse and swirl the colors into an interesting pattern with a wooden stir stick. To make the ringed pattern, alternate with two brushes holding ink and the rinsing agent onto the water sizing. The rinsing agent disperses the ink and you keep adding the ink and the rinsing agent until the entire surface is covered with colored rings. Gently blow the rings to create beautiful swirled patterns.

4. When you are happy with the design, print the marbled image by laying the paper gently on the surface of the water. Lift off immediately and lay face up onto the sheet of hard plastic or glass.

5. Take the paper print over to the sink and gently pour a glass of clean water over the print to wash away the sizing.

6. Lay the paper on a flat surface protected by freezer paper to dry. When completely dry, you can iron the sheet flat with a hot iron, no steam.

7. Before making your next piece of marbleized paper, skim the surface of the size with a newspaper strip to clean off the excess ink.

Simple ink marbling

Marbleized Paper with Oil Paint

This is a simple marbleizing technique, which produces a beautiful swirled colored paper. The thickened water supports the drops of paint so that the colors can mingle and disperse into infinite patterns. The oil marbleizing method is not as controlled as the seaweed marbleizing method but the results are just as spectacular as you peel the paper off the surface of the water. The only drawback is working with oil paints that require a bit more clean up and having to work with odorous turpentine.

Supplies You Will Need

Oil Paint

Tube oil paints that have been thinned to a creamy consistency with turpentine work best. Minimize the odor by using odorless turpentine available from art supply stores and paint stores. You can also use oil based enamel paints for this technique.

Paper

A good quality, medium weight paper works well. White-coated freezer or butcher paper can also be used. The paper will need to be cut to fit the inside of the roaster pan, 12" x 16".

Tools & Materials

Large, flat container: Use a 13" x 17" disposable tin foil roaster for this method and just wipe the paint off with paper towels for an easy, quick clean-up. Be sure that your pan is larger in size than your paper.

Package of unflavored gelatin: used to thicken the water.

Old newspapers: roughly cut into 6" x 13" strips. These strips are used to skim the surface of excess paint after a print has been made and to prepare the bath for the next piece.

Glass jars: for mixing the paint. Do not use plastic for this.

Wooden craft sticks: for mixing the paint.

Wooden skewers: for moving the paint around on the surface of the water.

Straw whisks: These are used to apply the paint to the water surface. You will need one for each color. These are easily made by cutting small bunches of straw from an old broom or a straw whisk brush. Tape the small bunches together with masking tape or hold together with rubber bands.

Sheet of hard plastic or glass: This should be at least 1" larger all around than your paper.

Workspace Tip: Organize your workspace close to a sink to rinse off the paper after the print has been made. Have everything close at hand for easy access. Have a large plastic garbage bag taped to the side of the table to dispose of the used newspaper strips.

continued page 50

Oil marbling

Decorating the Paper

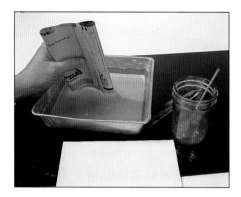

1. Prepare the water size by dissolving the package of gelatin in three cups of hot water. Pour the thickened water into the foil pan and add water until the water is three inches deep. Let the sizing sit for 1 hour before using. Just before adding the colors, shake the pan of size to release any bubbles and skim the surface with a newspaper strip to clean off any dust particles.

2. With a straw whisk dipped into the prepared color, drop the paint onto the water by holding the whisk 1" above the surface and gently tapping to release the paint. Keep tapping on the colors until the surface is covered. The color will appear faint on the water surface, but it will show up on the paper.

3. Create the swirled pattern by drawing the wooden skewer across the water surface, moving the colors around.

4. Print the marbled image by laying the paper gently on the surface of the water. Lift off immediately and lay face up onto the sheet of plastic or glass.

5. Take the paper print over to the sink and gently pour a glass of clean water over the print to wash away the size.

6. Lay the paper on a flat surface protected by freezer paper to dry. Depending on the amount of paint used, your prints should dry overnight. You can iron the sheet flat with a hot iron, no steam, when completely dry.

7. Before making your next piece of marbled paper, skim the surface of the size with a newspaper strip to clean off the excess paint.

8. For clean up, you can safely pour the size down the sink. Wipe the excess paint from the foil pan and save it for your next oil marbling session. This pan cannot be re-used for the ink or seaweed marbling technique after using it with the oil paints.

continued page 52

Oil marbling

Marbleized Paper Project

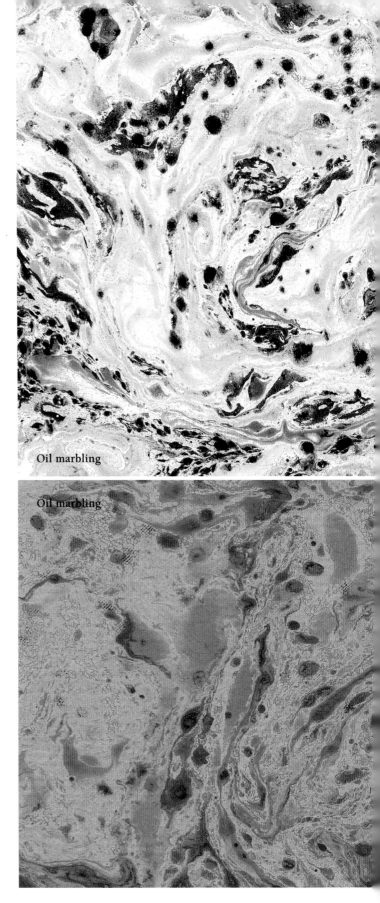

Oil marbling

Oil marbling

Coasters: Base paint the coasters with a maroon acrylic paint. Cover coasters with marbleized paper using decoupage finish and a foam brush. Finish with a resin coating. (See the section titled, "Ideas for Using Your Hand Decorated Papers" for instructions on applying a resin finish and for hints on applying papers to wooden coasters.)

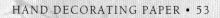

Oil marbling

Marbleized Paper with Seaweed

Seaweed marbleizing is the method of floating colors on a thick liquid and then transferring them to a sheet of paper. This method is the most complicated of all the marbling techniques but very rewarding when successful. The steps are a bit more complicated as you will need to mordant the paper, prepare the marbleizing size a day ahead, and carefully prepare the colors.

After you have done all this work, the process may not work. Temperature, humidity or the paints, sizing or paper not being prepared properly are all factors that will affect the results. This technique can be very temperamental, but if you are fortunate and it fully cooperates, beautiful images and patterns will be produced for your use in many projects. Traditionally, marbleized papers were used for the endpapers of the finest bound books. The origins of this craft started as early as the 8th century in Persia and the finest examples of marbleized papers are still found today in Turkey. Marbleizing was a closely guarded secret and created mysterious and traditionally named patterns such as "stone", "Get-gel", "Nonpareil" and "Fountain". It was also used to prevent tampering with what was written on it, like today's security papers. For example, the edges of accounting books were marbleized to make the removal of any pages easily seen.

Supplies You Will Need

Paint Color

You will obtain the best results with gouache or acrylic craft paints. Prepare the gouache (opaque watercolors in a tube form) by thinning with a little water. You may need to add a few drops of the photographic rinsing agent to the mixture to help the paints disperse on the surface of the size. The acrylic paints also need a few drops of water to thin them. Add a few drops of water at a time to your chosen paint and experiment on the size by dropping and testing that the paint disperses on the surface without sinking. If the paint sinks, it is too thick and needs a few more drops of water. If the paint expands out into a circle, then contracts, the color is too thick or the size and the color are too different in temperature.

Paper

The paper should be absorbent without a slick surface. A lightweight watercolor paper, a quality drawing paper or even copy paper will all work. Any paper that you choose must be prepared with an alum mordant (fixative) to help it hold the colored pattern. If you do not mordant the paper, the paint will wash away in the rinsing process. (See "Decorating the Paper" for instructions on preparing paper.)

Carrageenan Sizing

Carrageenan, also known as carragheen moss, is seaweed that is used to thicken foods such as ice cream. It can be found in art supply stores, health food stores and at beer making supply outlets where it is used to clarify the brew. It comes in a powdered form and is mixed with distilled water to make a thickened sizing for floating the colors upon. Add 2 Tablespoons of the powdered seaweed to 4 cups of distilled water. You can place it in a blender or hand whip to mix. Add more distilled water until the sizing is the consistency of thick gravy. You should have a depth of three inches in your marbleizing tray. Let the prepared sizing sit a day before using as the colors float better on a mature sizing.

Water Thickener

Use if you can't find carrageenan.

This product may be easier to find in your local craft shop than carrageenan. It has a base of carrageenan but has been further formulated into working with acrylic paints. The use of this product is recommended when using acrylic paints for your color. Mix the water thickener according to the package directions but use distilled water for the best results. Do not be afraid to add additional water to the thickener to make sure the consistency is right. Let this sit a day before using.

Other Tools & Materials

Alum: use to mordant the paper (treat with a fixative). It can be found at art supply stores and is different than the alum found in grocery stores used for pickling purposes

Large, flat container: A disposable tin foil roaster, a large plastic container or a photographic tray will all work for this method. Be sure your pan is larger than your paper.

Photographic rinsing agent: (available at photo supply stores) for helping stubborn colors to disperse on the water surface.

Old newspapers: roughly cut into 6" x 13" strips. These strips are used to skim the surface of excess paint after a print has been made and to prepare the bath for the next piece.

Plastic containers: for mixing the paint.

Wooden craft sticks: for mixing the paint.

Wooden skewers and simple rakes: for moving the paint around on the surface of the water. To make your own rakes, simply glue wooden skewers or round toothpicks onto the edge of a piece of corrugated cardboard. The corrugated sections will give you even spacing for different increments of the rake's teeth. Make rakes with the teeth set at 1", 1/2" and 1/4" apart. The rakes should easily fit into the tray's short end and will be used in both directions when combing through the floating paint to create the patterns.

Straw whisks: These are used for applying colors to the surface of the water. You will need one for each color. They are easily made by cutting small bunches of straw from an old broom or a straw whisk brush. Tape the small bunches together with masking tape or hold together with rubber bands.

Sheet of hard plastic or glass: This should be at least 1" larger all around than your paper.

Workspace Tip: Organize your workspace close to a sink to rinse off the paper after the print has been made. Have everything close at hand for easy access. Have a large plastic garbage bag taped to the side of the table to dispose of the used newspaper strips.

continued page 56

Seaweed marbling — "chevron"

Decorating the Paper

1. Prepare the alum mordant by dissolving two tablespoons alum with three cups of hot, distilled water. Mark one side of your paper with a small pencil mark in the corner and then turn over. The pencil mark will later help to determine which is the prepared side. With a clean sponge, sponge the cooled alum solution on the unmarked side. Stack these sheets and keep just damp in preparation to make a print of your marbled pattern.

2. Gently drop the prepared paint color onto the surface of the sizing with the straw whisks. The color should spread out on the surface of the sizing in a clean circle. If the color is sinking, or it does not spread, add a few more drops of water or rinsing agent to make it perform properly. You will need to experiment as all colors and brands react differently. The color will appear faint, but will print much brighter onto the white paper.

3. When the surface is covered with color, use a wooden skewer to swirl the color around to produce your design. You can also use the rakes to draw through the color. It will produce simple, combed designs. Comb the rake through the color in one direction, then the other to produce the fine nonpareil designs. Simply dropping the color onto the sizing in many splatters and then printing creates the traditional stone design.

4. Make the print by laying a sheet of your prepared paper over the sizing, with alum-prepared side down. Take care not to have any bubbles on the surface of the sizing or they will become large white spots on your finished design.

5. Remove the paper and place on the sheet of hard plastic or glass. It will not look great at this stage, as the excess sizing will need to be gently rinsed off.

6. Rinse the print by pouring a cup of clean water over the paper to remove the excess sizing. Rinse over a large bucket or the sink.

7. Before making your next print, skim the top of the sizing with a strip of newsprint to remove any left over color.

8. Hang the print or lay flat on freezer paper to dry. When completely dry, you can iron the paper sheet flat with a hot iron, no steam.

continued page 58

Seaweed marbling

Seaweed Marbleized Cards & Envelopes

Begin with a pre-purchased, plain paper card and envelope. Cut a square from the center of the front flap of each card. Cut a piece of seaweed marbled paper slightly larger than the square you cut out and glue it to the inside of each card so that it shows through the window you have cut. To finish the card, write a quote or message around the window with permanent ink. To decorate the envelope, cut a piece of seaweed marbled paper in a square and then cut a smaller square out of its center, leaving just the border. Glue the border with glue stick to the front of the envelope.

Seaweed Marbleized Paper Projects

Pillow Box: (See the section titled, "Making Envelopes & Boxes" for instructions and a pattern for the pillow parcel.) The package is made of seaweed marbled paper with a rubber-stamped label glued to the front. Secure ends of package with double-sided tape. Wrap package in a coordinating ribbon and secure ends of ribbon with a melted wax stamp.

Bookmarks: The bookmarks are made with pieces of seaweed marbled paper that are attached with glue stick to slightly larger pieces of cardstock. Punch a hole at the top of each bookmark and thread with a piece of gold cord.

Seaweed marbling — "nonpareil"

Nature Print Paper

This simple method uses nature as your design tool, pigment ink and any type of absorbent paper. Nature printing has been used by botanists and artisans throughout history for plant identification and decorative arts. Leonardo Da Vinci describes the process in his manuscript, Codex Atlanticus *complete with a printing of a sage leaf. There is a wonderful kit complete with all the materials, including the inks and paper, developed by Laura Donnelly Bethmann who has also authored a book filled with projects and step-by-step instructions for printing plants, feathers, fish and other natural objects.*

Supplies You Will Need

Ink

Use pigment ink in squeeze bottles. These are sold in rubber stamp stores as refill inks for pigment stamp pads.

Paper

Any paper that has a smooth surface is suitable. Do not use shiny, coated papers unless you plan to seal them with embossing powders.

Design Elements

Fresh leaves: Choose sturdy leaves with a strong vein pattern. Flatten your leaves in a heavy book one-half hour before you start printing, in order to make them easier to handle.

Other Tools & Materials

Dense, foam sponge wedges: to apply ink to leaf. You will need one for each color.

Tweezers: for lifting the leaves off of the paper.

Wax paper: cut into small 6" square pieces.

Plastic palette: to hold your color.

continued page 62

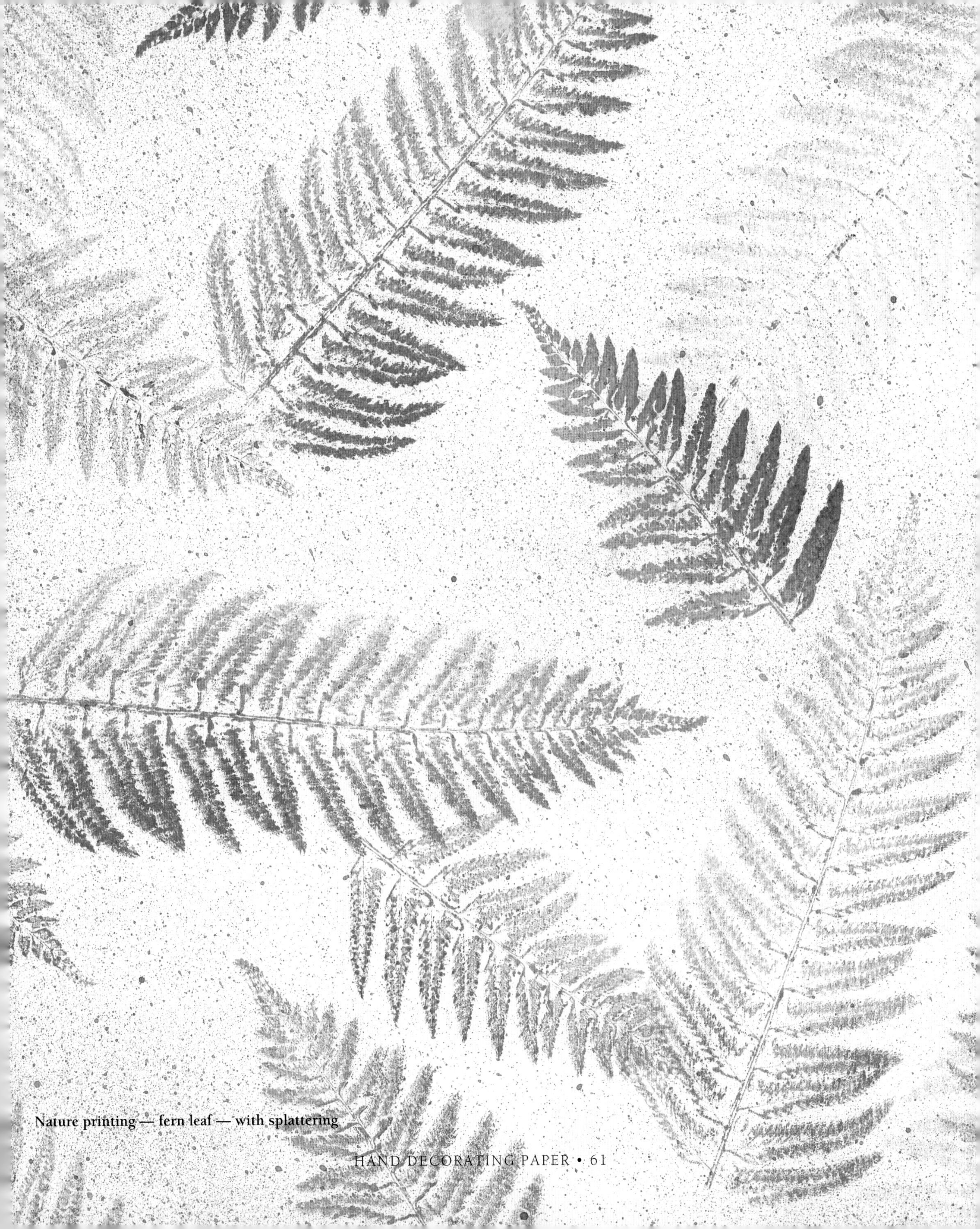

Nature printing — fern leaf — with splattering

Decorating the Paper

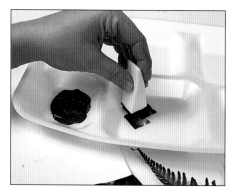

1. Squeeze a small amount of ink onto your palette. Dip the sponge wedge into the ink and pounce until you spread the ink out into a thin, even film on the sponge.

2. Carefully, sponge the paint on the underside of the leaf. If you are using more than one color, start with the lightest color first to prevent the colors from getting muddy.

3. Carefully, place the leaf down on the paper.

4. Place a sheet of clean wax paper over the leaves and smooth down gently with the heel of your hand.

5. Carefully, lift off the wax paper. Remove the leaves with the tweezers. Repeat until you are happy with your pattern.

Nature Print Paper Project

Leaf Gift Cards: Begin with a folded card. Attach a piece of brown art paper with torn edges to the front of the card with glue stick. Attach a slightly smaller piece of nature print paper to the front of this, so that the torn edges of the under paper peek out. Write a saying or quote on the front of the nature print paper with a permanent ink pen. 👑

Paste Paper

Paste papers are one of the easiest and most economical ways to produce beautiful, decorative papers. This ancient method of making designs in wet paste on paper is simple and interesting. You create papers that are rich in color, pattern and texture and that reflect the character of the maker.

Supplies You Will Need

Colored Paste

You will need a thick colored paste mixture which substitutes for your paint. Recipes for types of paste mixtures follow on page 65. Paste can be colored with a variety of mediums — acrylic paint, inks, powdered pigments, tube watercolor.

Paper

The best type of paper will be a sized paper that does not fall apart when wet. Many commercial printing papers or artist drawing papers will work well. You can also experiment with different surface textures and colored papers, such as shiny commercial printing coated paper or less expensive finger printing paper. The size of your paper will depend on the size of your hard plastic or glass surface, but a good size for beginners is 11" x 17".

Tools & Materials

Paste brushes: 1" to 2" flat, natural bristle paste brushes are the best for smoothing the paste evenly on the paper. You will need a brush for each color.
Plastic containers: for holding the mixed paste. Recycled margarine and yogurt containers work best.
Stir sticks: Wooden craft sticks are best for mixing the colored pigment into the paste.

Sponges: You will need several cellulose sponges.
Sheet of hard plastic or glass: Use as your working surface. This should be at least 1" larger all around than your paper. Shops that carry hard plastic or glass generally have an area with leftover pieces that are cheaper than having a piece cut from a large sheet.
Water: You will need a pan with about 3" of clean water for dipping the paper. The pan will need to be a bit larger than the paper you are using. This water will always be kept clean. You will also need a bucket of water for rinsing the sponges.
Tools for creating your designs: These can be rubber combs, plastic hair combs, sea sponges, rollers, kitchen utensils or anything else that will manipulate the paste into interesting designs and patterns.

Paste Recipes

There are three simple paste recipes. The wallpaper paste is by far the simplest, but you may prefer the cornstarch mixture. The cornstarch and flour mixture is the recipe used by many paste paper artists and will give a texture to the paper as well.

Wallpaper Paste:

Just add color pigment to a pre-mixed wallpaper paste mixture. The wallpaper paste will keep a long time and is always ready to add color and produce the papers.

Cornstarch Paste:

Combine 1/4 cup of cornstarch with 1/4 cup of cold water until well mixed. This will prevent lumps from forming. Add an additional one cup of water to the mix and heat over medium heat until the mixture resembles a thick custard. Keep stirring the mixture while cooking to prevent lumps. Add up to 1/2 cup more water if the mixture is too thick. Remove the mixture from the stove and stir occasionally while cooling. This paste will not keep long and is best used when fresh.

Flour & Cornstarch Paste:

2 Tablespoons corn starch   2 Tablespoons rice flour
1/2 teaspoon glycerin   2 1/2 - 3 cups water
Acrylic matte medium

Mix the dry ingredients and water until smooth. Bring the mixture to a boil, stirring constantly to avoid lumps. Once it boils, bring to a low heat and stir for a few minutes. The paste will thicken as it cools. Stir in the glycerin and allow the paste to cool. The glycerin is important as it makes the paste smooth and flexible when using the finished paper for bookbinding or for covering a box. Divide into plastic containers and when cool, add the same amount of acrylic matte medium so that you have a 1:1 ratio. You can store this paste in the refrigerator for a few days, but never freeze the mixture for future use.

continued page 66

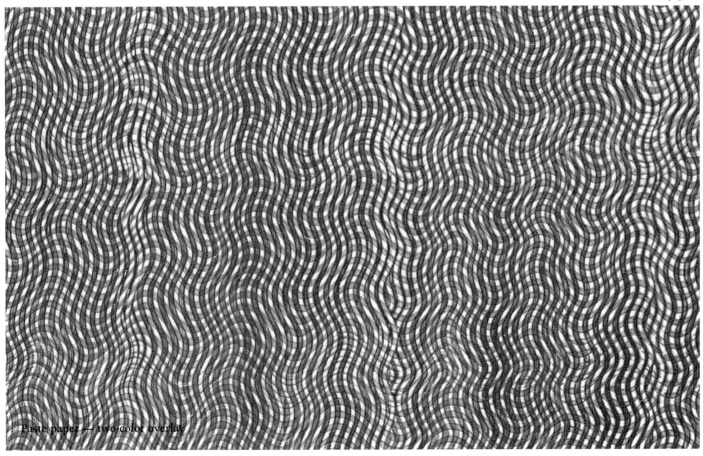

Paste paper — two-color overlay

Coloring the Paste

When the paste is cooled, add a small amount of a colored pigment. This can be acrylic paint, tube watercolors, inks, dry pigments or printing inks. Add small amounts of color at a time, as the paint will further thin out the paste. The color of the paste will be only a shade or two darker once it dries. To give the colored paste a metallic sheen when dry, mix in a 1/2 teaspoon of powdered gold pigment to each container.

Decorating the Paper

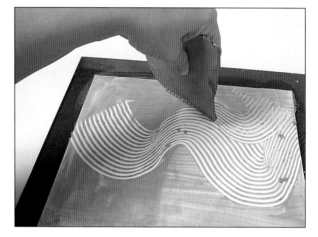

1. Have your water basins, sponges and tools ready. You will also need to have a line for hanging the papers up to dry or you can spread out large pieces of freezer paper to dry the papers flat.

2. Prepare the paper by wetting it first. Quickly dipping the paper in and out of the clean pan of water is the best way for an even wetting. Do not soak the paper, as doing so will eventually disintegrate it.

3. Lay the paper out onto the piece of hard plastic or glass and smooth it carefully with a clean, damp sponge to get rid of the excess water and remove any bubbles. The wet paper will stick tight to the smooth surface and will not wrinkle while you are working the paste.

4. Apply the colored paste as evenly as you can with the paste brush. Stroke the color on vertically, then horizontally for even coverage.

5. Add pattern and design using your imagination and a few tools. Cardboard pieces that have notches cut into the side, rubber combs used in decorative paint techniques, and fingertips or sponges are just a few. Be careful that the tools you use do not gouge too deeply into the paper causing it to tear.

6. Dry the paper by hanging on a rack or lying flat on a sheet of freezer paper. The paper will dry with curled edges but will glue flat when adhered to a surface. If you wish, smooth the paper with a hot iron, no steam. Be sure to use a pressing cloth to protect the surface while pressing.

Additional Paste Paper Techniques

Multi-Colored Paste Papers

Simply brush on more than one color of paste before making your designs and patterns. Blend the colors into each other carefully for a uniform pattern.

Print Overlay

Double printed papers display exquisite patterns that offer a complicated look by repeating the process over the top of a dried sheet. Make sure the first paste design is completely dry and re-dip it into the clean water bath. Brush on a new color and proceed to add a design over the initial pattern.

Pulled Paste Paper

Pulled paste paper is produced by painting colored paste on two sheets of paper and then laying them face to face. Smooth the top paper down gently with your hand then, carefully and slowly pull the papers apart. If the papers are difficult to pull apart, try using a little less paste on the surfaces. The papers will have a feathery design and the two sheets will be identical.

Printed Paste Paper

Printed paste paper is produced when you create the design in the paste on a smooth surface, such as the hard plastic or glass sheet. Then the paper is placed on top of the paste where the print is made. This method is perfect for producing a paste design on delicate or inexpensive papers that would disintegrate if dipped into the water bath. It also gives a distinctive look to the paste design and is a good method to try with children.

1. Spread the colored paste evenly over the surface of the hard plastic or glass using the paste brushes and create the design by manipulating the paste with your chosen tools.

2. Lower the paper onto the paste-covered surface and gently pat the back of the paper to transfer the design.

3. Lift the paper and hang or lay flat to dry.

continued page 68

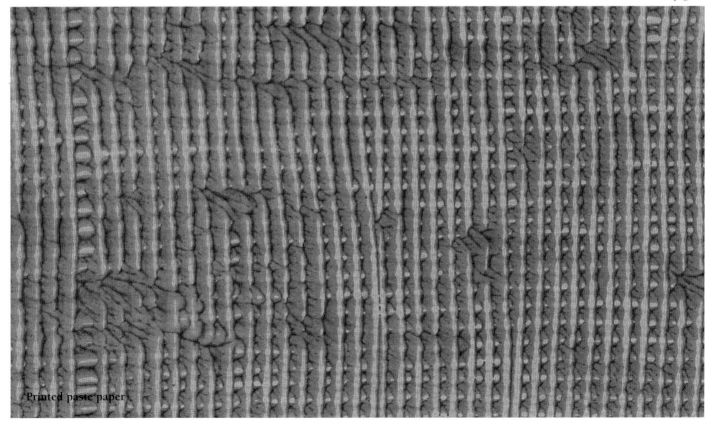

Printed paste paper.

Paste Paper Projects

Triangle Box: The parcel is made with printed paste paper and accented with rubber stamped labels in Asian motifs. (See section titled, "Making Envelopes & Boxes" for instructions and a pattern for the triangle package.)

Spiral-Bound Album: The cover of this album is adorned with pieces of paste paper and a hand-cut block printed motif. (See section titled "Block Printing by Cutting Your Own Blocks" for instructions on cutting your own blocks and printing them on paper.)

Triangle Accordion Journal: Both sides of the book are covered in paste paper. Finishing is the addition of a piece of art paper and a bee trinket. The book is held closed by gold elastic cord.

Garden-Theme Journal: Both sides of the book are covered in paste paper. Finishing is the addition of pieces of torn, garden-theme papers and a bee trinket. The book is held closed by gold elastic cord.

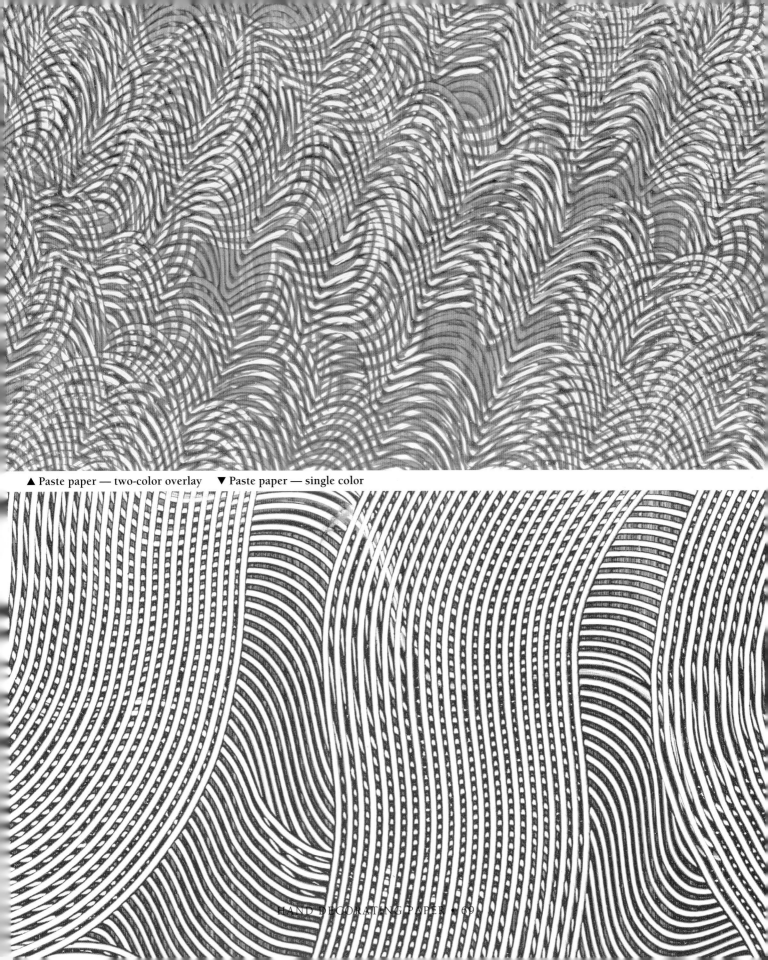

▲ Paste paper — two-color overlay   ▼ Paste paper — single color

Rubber Stamped Paper

The method of rubber-stamping has grown into a beautiful art form with many wonderful techniques. The range of motifs available in rubber stamps is huge. Whatever motif or theme you are looking for, there will be a stamp available!

Supplies You Will Need

Stamp Pad Inks

The stamp pad inks come in a vast array of colors and most are acid free and safe for memory albums and journals. The inks are poured onto a stamp pad, and the pad is used to apply color to the rubber stamp. Make sure your stamp pad has a raised pad so it can be used on any size of stamp. Most stamp pads have ink already in them.

Paper

Any type of paper is suitable for this method.

Rubber Stamps

Used to stamp patterns on the paper, the stamps are available in small sizes that can be repeated for a design, or in larger sizes for instant coverage.

Decorating the Paper

1. Load the stamp evenly with the ink by lightly tapping the stamp on the inkpad.
2. Press the stamp firmly onto the surface without rocking the stamp. Practice on a scrap piece of paper to master the skill of perfect stamping before moving to your project.
3. Gently lift stamp to reveal the resulting image.

Additional Rubber Stamping Techniques

Rubber-stamping with bleach creates beautiful, muted images. The color of the motif comes out a lighter shade than the paper it is stamped on. Use full strength household bleach that has been poured onto a piece of felt in a disposable plate. Dab your stamp onto the felt to load bleach onto the rubber stamp. Then stamp this onto the paper. Handmade papers in different colors seem to work the best, but it will work on any colored paper. Stamp with the bleach and watch the image magically appear. Wash your stamps immediately after use to prevent damage.

continued page 72

Rubber stamped with antiquing

Rubber Stamped Paper Projects

▲ **Memory Journal:** Begin with a pre-purchased journal. Attach a piece of faux leather paper to the top with craft glue. On top of this, attach a slightly smaller piece of paper that has been rubber stamped with bleach. The finishing touches are a vertical strip of the faux leather paper, an antiqued photocopied label, a torn circle of art paper and a bee charm.

▶ **Cornucopia Box:** This hand-made paper is antiqued with tea then rubber stamped. Laminate the paper onto a heavy card stock to make the parcel sturdy. (See "Laminating Paper" for instructions on this technique.) Fold the paper into package shape and secure with double-sided tape. (See section titled, "Making Envelopes & Boxes" for instructions and a pattern for the cornucopia package.) Finish with gold ribbon and a wax stamp. 🖐

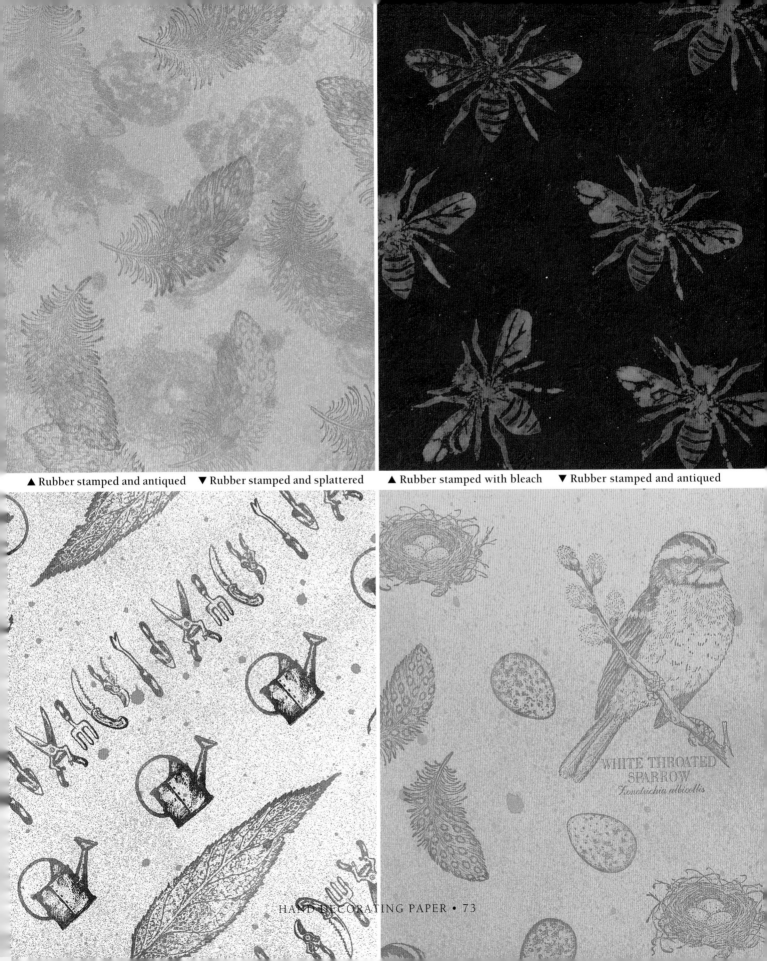

▲ Rubber stamped and antiqued   ▼ Rubber stamped and splattered   ▲ Rubber stamped with bleach   ▼ Rubber stamped and antiqued

WHITE THROATED
SPARROW
Zonotrichia albicollis

Splattered Paper

Splattering is a paint technique that can make interesting papers quickly and easily. This technique works well with other methods including nature printing, stenciling, resist and watercolor washes.

Supplies You Will Need

Paint

Acrylic paint is the medium most often used. You may prefer a mixture of one part acrylic paint to one part acrylic extender. Water can also be used to thin the color. You can also use thinned down colored paste (the same recipe given for the "Paste Paper" method) to splatter on your papers.

Paper

Any type of paper can be used for this decorative painting method.

Tools & Materials

Splattering tool: for dispersing the paint.
Large, stiff bristled brush: for dispersing the paint.
Palette knife: for pulling across the brush. A heavy card can also be used.
Workspace Tip: One drawback to this technique is that it can be messy. Use a large piece of freezer paper to protect your work surface before attempting this treatment.

Decorating the Paper

There are two techniques you can use. The first method uses a large, stiff brush and the second uses a splattering tool designed for this technique. For both methods the consistency of the paint is important, not too thick or too thin

1. *Using the brush method:* Dip the tips of the brush into the color, taking care not to add too much paint or it will fall onto your paper in large globs. Use a piece of heavy card or palette knife to stroke over the bristles of the brush, directing the spatters of paint towards the paper surface. Pull the card towards you or you will end up splattered. Add more colored splatters as needed. Let the paint dry before adding a second splattered coat of a different color if desired.
2. *Using a splattering tool:* This tool has a stiff bristled end and a moveable wooden handle with a metal bar to move through the bristles to form the splatters. You can control the splatters more easily and it is much quicker than the brush method. Fill the bristles with paint, turn the handle and watch the specks, dots and splatters quickly fly onto the paper surface.

continued page 76

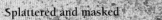
Splattered and masked

Additional Splattered Paper Techniques

Mask the splatters and create interesting patterns on your paper by placing pressed leaves, keys or any other object onto your paper surface to mask the paint. Let the paint dry, reposition the objects and then splatter with another color. The design can be built up using this technique to create an uncommonly attractive paper with rich depth.

Splattered Paper Project

Triangle Accordion Journal: Cover both sides of the book with sponged paper that has been splattered with metallic gold paint. Attach star and bird charms with hot glue. The book is held together with gold elastic cord.

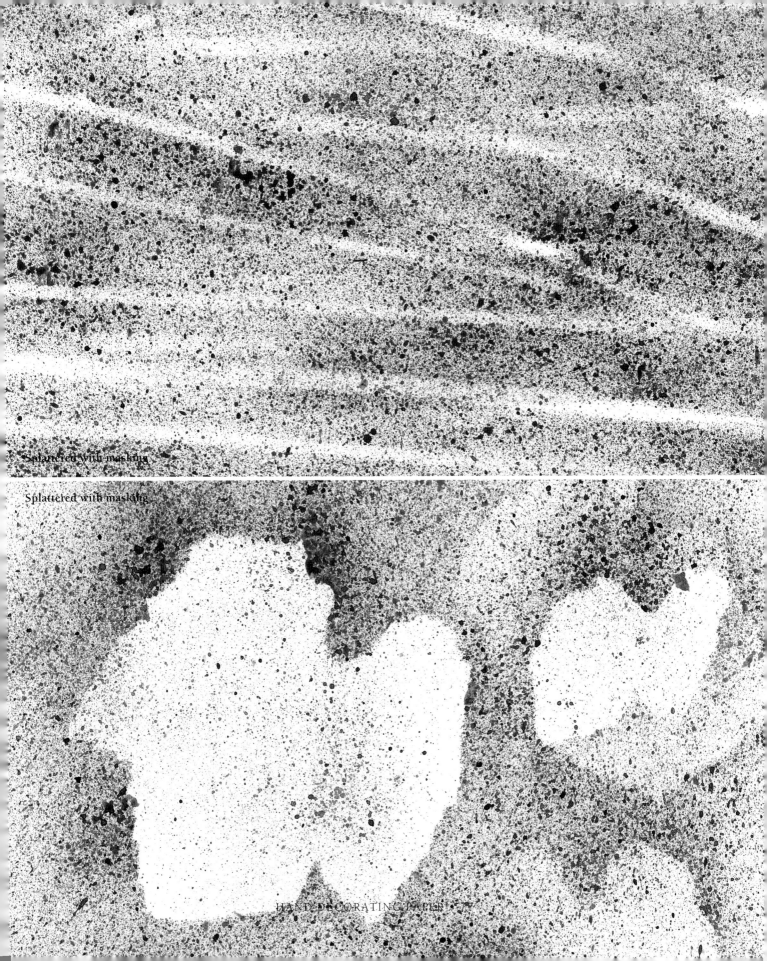

Splattered with masking

Splattered with masking

HAND-DECORATING PAPER · 79

Sponged Paper

You can create soft, fascinating patterns with this sponging technique. The goal is to achieve a piece of paper with a colorful and interesting surface. Use acrylic craft paint, a natural sea sponge and different colors of pastel paper to make this decorative paper. Used in combination with other methods such as block printing or paint resist, sponging helps to soften the overall effect.

Supplies You Will Need

Paint

Acrylic craft paints or gouache work best for this technique.

Paper

Any paper will do for this method. Experiment with a colored pastel paper or a good quality drawing paper.

Sponges

Sea Sponge: Choose your sponges carefully. Every sponge has a unique surface for a variety of sponged appearances.
Compressed Sponges: These flat cellulose sponges are easily cut into different shapes for sponging a pattern onto your paper. The sponge will expand to a regular thickness when placed in water.

Other Materials

Palette: for holding the paint.
Workspace Tip: Cover your workspace with freezer paper as you will go up to and over the paper edges as you work. After each sheet of paper is decorated, wipe the paint off the freezer paper before placing down the next sheet.

continued page 80

Sponged paper with compressed sponge overlay

Decorating the Paper

1. Dampen the sponge with water and squeeze out the excess. Pour paint onto a palette.
2. Dip the sponge into the paint and work the paint up into the sponge by tapping on a paper towel. You do not want too much paint on your sponge or the pattern will be too harsh.

3. Lightly pounce the sponge on the paper surface with a tapping motion to create the decorative surface.
4. Use a variety of colors. There is no need to completely cover the surface. Let a bit of the paper color show through for interest.

5. Try cutting a compressed cellulose sponge into an interesting shape for sponging a pattern onto your paper. Sponge the paper all over before adding a decorative sponged pattern.

Sponged Paper Projects

Square Pinwheel Envelope: The envelope is made by combining sponged and stamped paper with gold wrapping paper. (See section titled, "Making Envelopes & Boxes" for instructions on making a square pinwheel envelope.) Secure the four points with a length of black ribbon and stamped gold wax.

Wrapping Paper & Card: This whimsical box is wrapped with diamond sponged paper and a large, sheer ribbon bow with plastic fruit on top. The card is sponged to match. A pear cut from a plastic eraser is used to stamp the front. 🖋

▲ Sponged paper with compressed sponge overlay   ▼ Sponged paper

Spray Painted Paper

This technique has you producing large sheets of awe-inspiring papers easily and quickly. It is a wonderful method for making your own giftwrap. Because you are using spray paint, make sure your work area is protected and properly ventilated.

Supplies You Will Need

Paint

Spray paints are used in this technique. Try to find acrylic-based sprays for use on paper. Metallic sprays look dynamic on brown paper and pastel colors can be used on white paper for softer romantic looks.

Paper

For this method use the brown paper rolls for wrapping parcels and rolls of cartridge paper or paper used for covering tables. Any other paper will also work for this unique method.

Other Materials

Iron for pressing the paper flat after technique is completed.

Workspace Tip: Cover your workspace with freezer paper making sure you cover all areas that could get sprayed. Make sure you are spraying in a well-ventilated area.

Decorating the Paper

Crinkled Design

1. Crinkle up the sheet of paper and unfold slightly.

2. Place the paper on a protected surface and spray at a low angle, spraying across the paper to capture the wrinkles and folds. You can spray with additional colors from different angles for a multi-colored paper.

3. When the paper is dry, flatten with a hot iron, no steam. The results will be a three-dimensional crinkled look on a flat piece of paper.

Folded Design

1. Fold the paper into 1" accordion folds. Place on your workspace, with the paper loosely unfolded.

2. Spray paint from a low angle in one direction only, facing the folds. Let dry completely.

3. Flatten the paper with your hands and fold 1" accordion folds at a right angle to the first folds. Repeat the spraying step.

4. When dry, flatten the paper with a hot iron, no steam. The resulting pattern will be an elegant three-dimensional design. Experiment with different folds, spraying angles and colors to create an endless array of patterns and designs.

continued page 84

Spray painted paper

Spray painted paper — folded design

Paper Project

Frame: Begin with a pre-purchased cardboard frame. Attach pieces of sprayed paper with decoupage finish and a foam brush. Add pieces of torn, stenciled paper and other solid art papers on top of the sprayed paper. To finish, attach metal charms with hot glue.

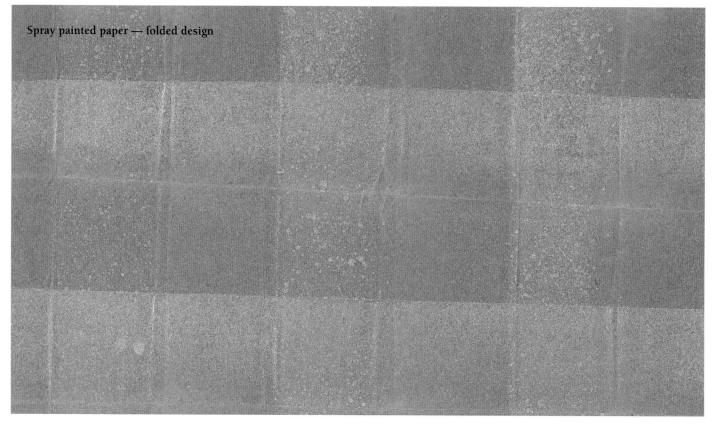

Spray painted paper — folded design

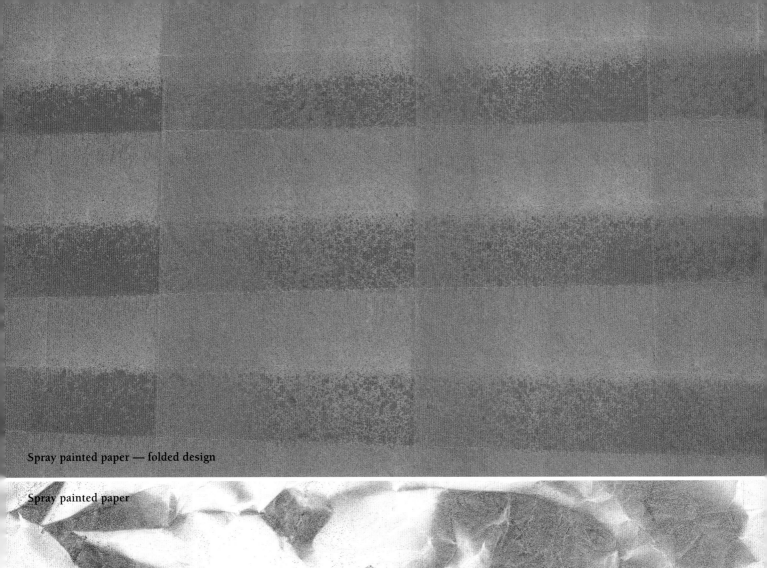

Spray painted paper — folded design

Spray painted paper

Stenciled Paper

Stenciling designs is a fast and easy way to decorate your paper. There are hundreds of stencils available on the market in a wide array of motifs. Experiment with roller stenciling when working on large pieces of paper for very quick results.

The roller stenciling technique was developed and perfected by stencil master Sandra Buckingham, whose fresh approach to stenciling and her many books on the subject have made the craft accessible to everyone. The most important thing to remember when stenciling on paper with any type of paint is to use a very small amount of paint for best results. If your paint is leaking under the stencil, you are using too much!

Supplies You Will Need

Paint

Use a waterbased stencil gel or acrylic craft paint for your stencil designs. If using acrylic paint add a few drops of extender to the palette to prevent your paint from drying out too quickly.

Paper

Any paper is suitable for stenciling, from rough handmade papers to glossy, sheer vellums.

Stencils

Use single cut stencils cut from stencil plastic for best results. All the stencil designs presented in this book are by Sandra Buckingham.

Other Tools & Materials

Dense, sponge rollers: These work best for applying the paint quickly and efficiently.
Flat palette: or sheet of hard plastic or glass.
Palette knife: or plastic putty knife for spreading the paint.
Paper towels: for absorbing excess paint.

continued page 88

Stenciled paper — all over design

Decorating the Paper

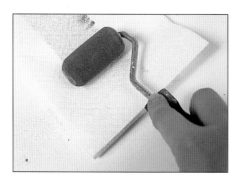

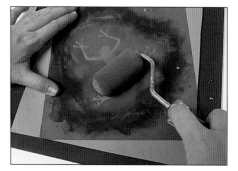

1. Squeeze the paint onto the pallet and smooth down with the palette knife.
2. Roll the roller over the paint, spreading it out evenly and working the paint into the roller. Use immediately and do not let the paint dry on the palette.
3. Roll the roller onto a pile of paper towels to remove any excess paint that could leak under the stencil. You do not want an excess of paint on the roller or it will seep under the cut area of stencil.
4. Hold the stencil in place with your hand or tape. Roll the paint over the motif making sure you do not roll over the edges. You will be able to stencil many motifs before you have to pick up more paint with the roller.
5. Lift the stencil to reveal the finished

design. Stencil the motifs in a planned pattern or an all over random pattern.

Stenciled Paper Projects

Fern Table Mat: Cover wooden, oval mat with stenciled fern paper. Seal top with a protective resin coating. (See section titled, "Ideas for Using Your Hand Decorated Papers" for instructions on applying a resin coating and for hints on applying papers to wooden tablemats.) Glue thin cork to the underside of the mat to protect the table surface.

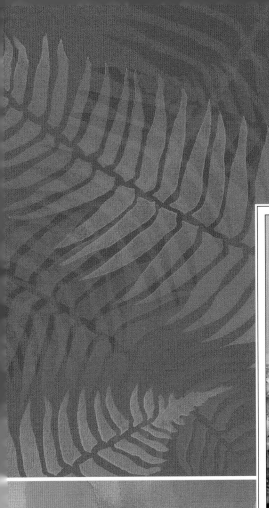

Sun Cylinder Lantern: Stencil suns onto handmade rice paper. Decoupage paper onto the glass cylinder with decoupage finish. Finish by sealing with a coat of acrylic matte varnish. Adorn with gold ribbon, charms, gold curly filament and velvet leaves. Insert a candle to create an attractive lantern.

Four samples of roller stenciling

Tie-Dye Paper

This technique is actually an ancient Japanese paper treatment called orizomegami. In Japan, the decoration of paper has reached a cultural and traditional importance with a high level of quality and craftsmanship. This is one of the easiest and most effective techniques. You may remember doing this technique in kindergarten with paper towels and food coloring. The magic of unfolding the paper and revealing the beautiful patterns is still exciting.

Supplies You Will Need

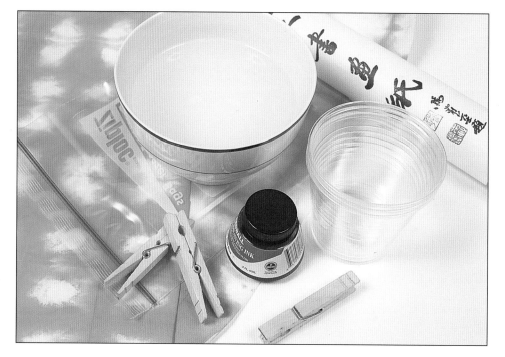

Inks

Use good quality drawing inks that have been diluted with water in a 1:1 ratio. You can also use the inks full strength for a more vibrant paper.

Paper

The paper needs to be thin, soft and absorbent without any added sizes or coatings. Japanese rice paper works best, but you can also use mulberry paper.

Other Tools & Materials

Clean water: You will need only a small bowl.
Plastic containers: to hold the inks. Disposable cups or recycled plastic containers work well.
Wooden clothespins: for holding the folded paper closed.
Plastic sandwich bags: for squeezing out excess water and ink.
Plastic gloves: to protect your hands from ink stains.

continued page 92

Tie-dye paper

Decorating the Paper

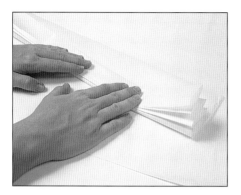

1. Fold the paper in even, accordion pleats along the length of the paper.

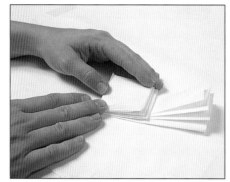

2. Accordion fold again down the length of the strip. Fold in squares, rectangles or triangles to create different looks. Use a clothespin to hold the folded paper together.

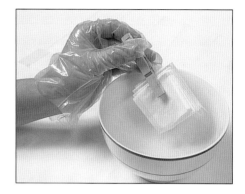

3. Dip the folded paper into the bowl of clean water, squeezing out the excess.

4. Starting with the lightest colors, dip the corners into the inks. Working from the lightest to the darkest colors keeps your inks from becoming muddy. Do not hold the corners in the ink too long or it will color too much of the paper.

5. Place the folded paper inside a plastic sandwich bag. Squeeze the folded paper to help the inks spread and to remove the excess ink. You can rinse out the plastic bag and reuse it for any additional tie-dye papers.

6. Carefully, unfold the paper pleat by pleat. The wet paper can easily tear, so go slowly and with care. Place the unfolded sheet on freezer paper to dry flat or drape over a line to dry. When dry, carefully flatten the paper with a hot iron, no steam.

Tie-dyed papers

Watercolor Paper

Watercoloring a piece of paper simply puts a wash of sheer color on the paper. However, there are some additional interesting techniques given here that can be used alone or in combination with one another to create easy, yet sensational, decorative papers.

Supplies You Will Need

Paint

Artist quality watercolors and gouache (an opaque watercolor paint) work best, but watered down acrylic paints or water-soluble fabric paints are also usable in this technique. To add a metallic sheen to your watercolor papers, mix a little gold powdered pigment with a 1:1 mix of liquid gum arabic (available in art stores and health food stores) and water. Place this mixture in a plastic spray bottle and spray onto the washed on colors.

Paper

Lightweight watercolor paper that has been stretched (directions follow) is the best for this technique, but you can also use a good quality drawing paper or even copy paper with varying results.

Other Tools & Materials

A selection of soft brushes: for laying down the colors. Artist quality brushes are best, but large, soft craft brushes will also work.

Plastic spray bottles: Optional techniques — you can also use plastic spray bottles filled with watered down paint to spray the paper with color.

Sheet of hard plastic or glass: to be used as a working surface. This should be at least 2" larger all around than the size of the paper you wish to decorate.

Brown paper gummed tape: for stretching the paper.

Water: You will need a pan with about 3" of clean water for dipping the paper. The pan will need to be a bit larger than the paper you are using.

Palette: for mixing and diluting the paint colors.

continued page 96

Water color paper

Decorating the Paper

1. **Stretching the Paper:** You will need to stretch or size your paper before working on it or the water will create wrinkles and curling, which is difficult to work with. Stretch the watercolor paper by dipping it into the clean water and lying flat on a sheet of hard plastic or glass. Cut four pieces of brown paper tape, each piece about 2" longer than each side of the paper. Dip the tape into water and squeegee off the excess by running through two fingers. Adhere each side of the paper down to the hard plastic or glass with the tape and sponge lightly to remove any excess water. Let dry completely. You can speed up this drying process with a hair dryer. Re-wet the paper before decorating with the colors by sponging or spraying with clean water.

2. Place your colors in the palette and mix with water to obtain a thin consistency. You can wet your stretched paper or apply the color to dry paper. Washing the color onto dry or wet paper produces two very different looks.

3. Wash or spray on a variety of colors but beware of using too many hues, as they will get muddy when mixed together. Keep to the same color families for the best results. For example, blues and purples together or reds and oranges together.

4. Let the colored paper dry before removing from the hard plastic or glass sheet with an art knife.

Additional Watercolor Techniques

Salting

This decorative technique is used by watercolor artists and silk painters to obtain an interesting design in the washed on colors. Use watercolors or gouache, watercolor paper and coarse salt.

1. Water down your paint to an inky consistency and brush or spray over the paper. Aim for a washed effect with a variety of shades of the color.

2. Sprinkle the salt over the surface while the paint is still wet. You must wait until the paint has *dried completel* before rubbing off the salt and revealing the mottled surface. The salt, on the damp paper absorbs the color, leaving a fascinating dappled design in a variety of shades.

Cracked Technique

This patterned watercolor technique is easily produced with kitchen plastic wrap, watercolors and watercolor paper.

1. Thin paint to an inky consistency and brush over the paper. Aim for a washed effect with a variety of shades of the color.

2. While the paint is still quite damp, place a piece of plastic wrap on top.

3. Move the plastic wrap around to create a cracked look in the wet paint. You must wait until the paint has *dried completely* before taking off the plastic wrap and revealing the cracked surface. The wet paint pools around the folds and wrinkles to produce the abstract fractured pattern.

Watercolor Paper Project

Triangle Accordion Journal: The book is covered front and back with salted watercolor paper. Finishing is the addition of torn pieces of art paper and ocean trinkets. Write your favorite quote around the edges of the papers. The book is held together with silver elastic cord. ☝

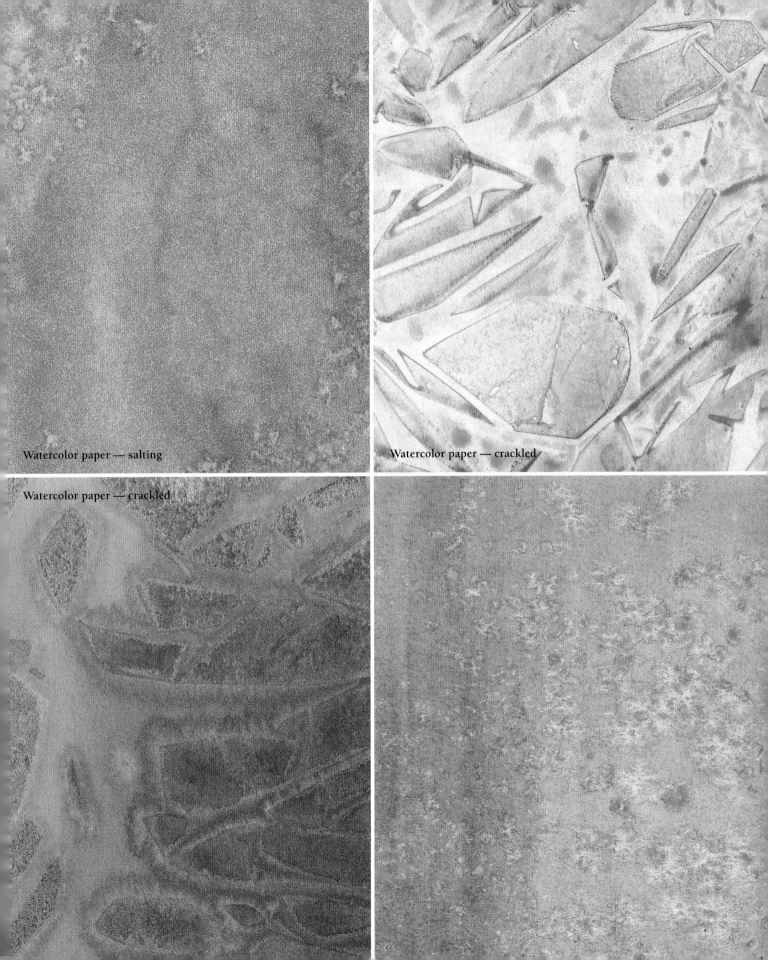

Watercolor paper — salting

Watercolor paper — crackled

Watercolor paper — crackled

Ideas for Using Your Hand Decorated Papers

There are an infinite number of extraordinary gifts and projects you can make with your decorated papers. The ideas in this book demonstrate only a few of the items you can make for the home or for presenting as gifts.

Bookbinding

Gift Tags & Cards

Gift tags and cards not only identify your presents, they also enhance the gift-wrapping. The best cards and tags match the decorative paper wrappings. Hand decorated papers can be used to make beautiful cards and tags, even when unadorned. Adhere the papers to the cards with a solid glue stick or with double-sided tape. Adorn your cards, if you wish, with charms, sayings or rubber-stamped images.

Decorative paper for covering boards to make your own journals and scrapbooks should be light to medium in weight. If the paper is too heavy the covering will be difficult. Paste papers, printed papers, and marbleized papers make wonderful coverings. Traditionally marbleized papers were used for the endpapers in handsome leatherbound books. Small pieces of decorative papers can also be used to create collages on pre-constructed journals.

Frames

Decorative papers can be used to cover mat boards and wooden frames to create wonderful accents for rooms and to show off cherished photographs. Use light to medium weight papers that have been decorated using the method of your choice. The best way to adhere the papers to the mat board or wooden frame is to use decoupage finish and a foam brush. See page 108 for a frame stand pattern.

Glass Cylinders

Glass cylinders can make impressive lanterns when filled with water and a floating candle. Lightweight papers are the best for this method, as the light from the candle makes the paper glow and show off the decorative covering. Simply cut the decorative paper to the size of your cylinder and adhere to the outside of the cylinder with decoupage finish. When dry, brush on a protective coating of acrylic matte varnish.

The pre-historic-looking cylinder lantern shown here is covered with stenciled paper. Raffia, buttons and copper leaves have been attached with hot glue.

Protecting Your Projects with a Resin Coating

A resin, pour-on coating gives projects a hard, waterproof finish that imparts a depth and luster equal to 50 coats of varnish. Not only does it give a professional finish, but also a practical, easy to clean surface. Trays, coasters, tablemats, decorative plates, ornaments and vases all benefit from this durable glossy finish. The steps are easy to follow and the results are spectacular.

Supplies You Will Need

Pour-on Resin: You will want the type that comes in two parts, the resin and the hardener. You will mix only as much as you can use on your project, as it cannot be saved for other projects. The resin has a unique self-leveling quality that is attained only by using enough to flood the surface. It is better to mix too much rather than too little. A four-ounce kit will cover up to 1 square foot.

Mixing cup: for mixing the resin. Use a disposable container.

Wooden stir stick: for stirring the resin. Plan to discard this after use.

Disposable foam brush: or glue brush for applying the resin.

Thin, white glue: for decoupaging the paper to the wooden surface.

Rubber cement or masking tape: for protecting the bottom of your project from drips.

Instructions

1. **Prepare your workspace:** You will need to protect your surface with freezer paper or wax paper and use plastic cups to prop up your project and keep it off of the working surface. The working surface should be level and the area warm and free from dust.
2. **Prepare project surface:** Adhere your decorative paper to the surface of the item. Seal the decorated paper with a coating of white glue that dries clear. Allow to dry thoroughly. Your project surface should be dry and free of any dust or grease. The coating will drip off the sides of the project, so you can protect the underside by brushing on some rubber cement or lining the bottom edges with masking tape. If drips occur on an unprotected surface, they can be sanded off when the finish has cured.
3. **Mix resin:** Measure out the two parts in the same container. You want to mix exactly one part resin with one part

▲ **Prehistoric Table Mat:** *The wooden rectangular mat is covered with a paste paper, torn stenciled paper and tissue paper collage. A protective coating of a two-part resin covers the top and thin cork is glued to the underside to protect the table surface.*

hardener. Mix the resin and hardener with the wooden stick until thoroughly blended. Mixing will be completed after a full two minutes of vigorous mixing. The importance of thorough mixing cannot be over-emphasized as poor mixing can result in a soft finish. Do not be concerned if bubbles get whipped into the mixture. The bubbles will be removed after the resin is poured.

4. **Apply resin:** As soon as the resin is mixed, pour over the surface of your project. Spread the resin where necessary, using the brush. You will have about 10 minutes to work on your project before it begins to set up.
5. **Allow to dry:** After about 5 minutes, the air bubbles created when mixing will rise to the surface. They can be broken by gently "huffing" on them until they disappear. Avoid inhaling the fumes while you pop the bubbles. It is the carbon dioxide in your breath that breaks ups the bubbles. Allow your project to cure for a full 72 hours to a hard and permanent finish. Discard the mixing cup, the stir stick and the resin brush.

Covering Wooden Boxes, Coasters & Tablemats

Wooden boxes, coasters and tablemats can all be covered with your handmade decorative papers. Heavy to lightweight papers will all work for this application. Apply the paper with decoupage finish and a foam brush. To create a perfect fit when applying decorative paper to a wooden plaque, tray, coaster or other wooden surface, you will want to use the following method.

1. Cut the paper at least 1/2" larger all around than the top of your surface.
2. Apply decoupage finish to the back of the paper or the item surface using a sponge brush. Be sure the surface is well covered. Position paper and smooth down with a brayer or your fingertips. Wipe off any residue with a damp cloth. Let dry completely.
3. Hold a piece of sandpaper at a 45-degree angle to the edge of the surface and sand the paper until it cuts through. Be sure not to scratch the top of your paper. This method gives a very precise and professional looking edge and requires no guess work in cutting the image exactly to the size of the surface.
4. Finish by covering paper surface with decoupage finish or a resin coating for protection.

▲ **Wooden box pictured:** Begin with a pre-purchased wooden box. Base paint the box with black acrylic craft paint. Decoupage the box top with a paper decorated with block printing. Complete the box top by sealing it with a resin coating. 🖌

Making Envelopes & Boxes

There is always a time when you need a pretty box for presenting a gift, and it will mean a great deal more if you make it yourself. You can find lots of templates and box makers to construct your own boxes and parcels of varying shapes and sizes in craft shops and rubber stamp outlets. They are all easily made with careful cutting and scoring. The paper should be a heavy card stock, and the larger the box, the heavier the paper should be. If your decorative paper has been constructed of a lightweight or medium weight paper, you will need to adhere it to a heavier paper. Use decoupage finish and a wide brush to laminate the sheets together. When dry,

you can iron any wrinkles with a hot iron, no steam.

When constructing a new box shape, make it first with plain copy paper to be sure you have the dimensions and size correct before you use your good decorative papers. Do the extra work to make a plastic template. Trace the parcel design onto a sheet of clear, heavy plastic with a permanent pen so you can simply trace around the design on the back of your decorative paper to save time and to make perfect decorative parcels. After tracing your pattern, cut along the solid lines and score on the dotted lines with a stylus or bone folder. Use double-sided tape to adhere your boxes and parcels together when cut out and scored.

The triangle box is an attractive shape for packaging charming trinkets such as jewelry, scarfs, or even candy. The Paste Paper technique was used to decorate the paper. The technique was done on a heavier card stock paper so that it would make a sturdy box. Chinese emblems were glued to the box to make this an exotic-looking package. See page 106 for the triangle box pattern.

◄ *This box shown was made using the Marbleized Paper with Seaweed technique. A square of paper was Rubber Stamped and glued to the box for a label. A ribbon and a wax seal completes this pretty package. See page 105 for the pillow box pattern.*

▶ *Unusual-shaped boxes make gifts even more special. And if you have decorated the paper used for the box — you can personalize it for the gift recipient. This cornucopia box has a romantic feeling. The paper used to make the box was rubber stamped with a word stamp. A ribbon and a wax seal finishes the effect. See page 104 for the cornucopia box pattern.*

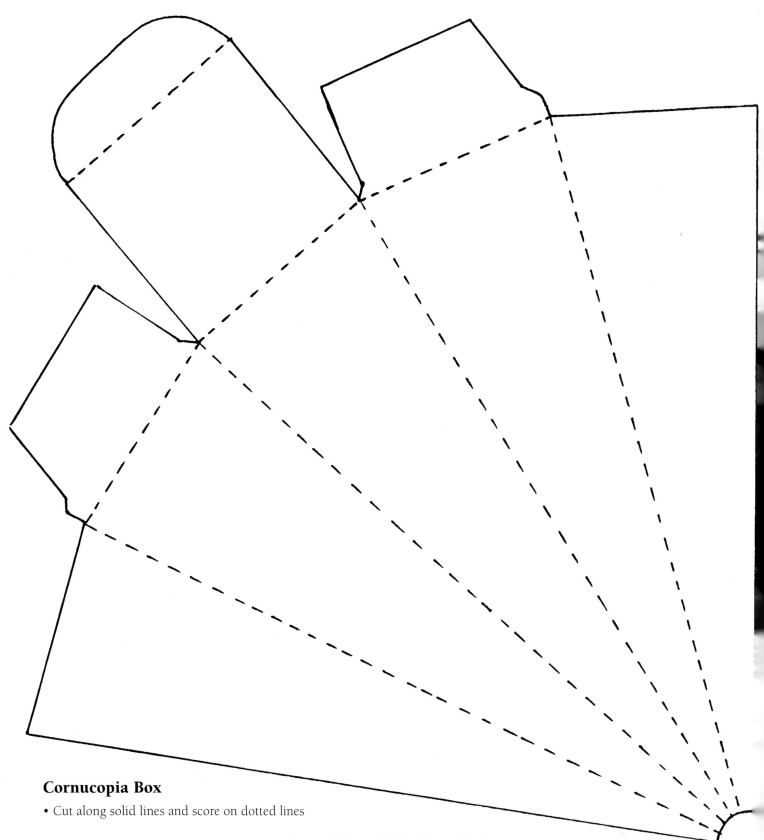

Cornucopia Box

• Cut along solid lines and score on dotted lines

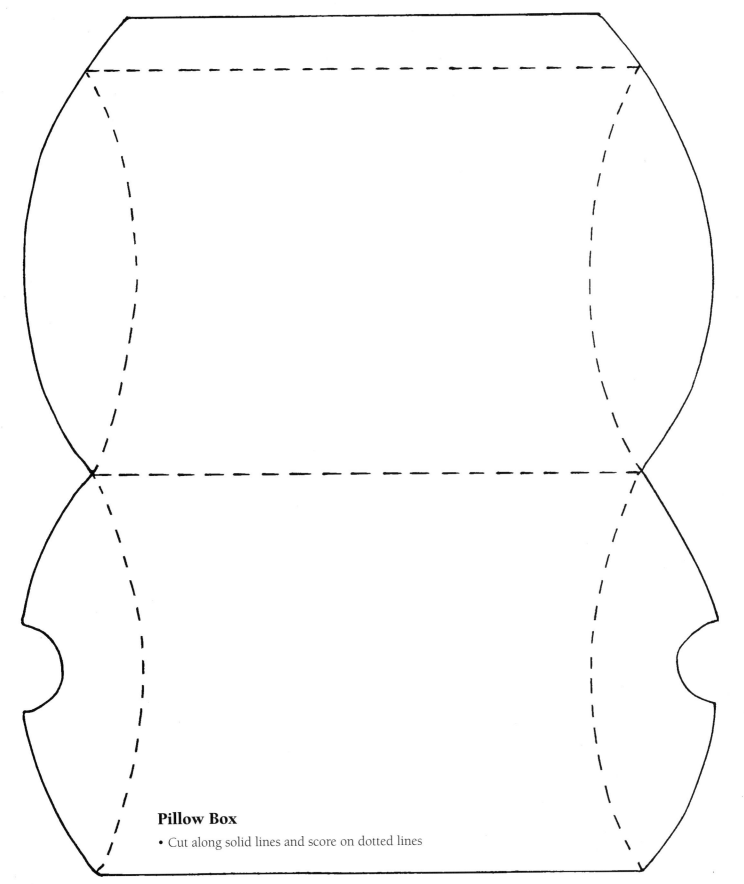

Pillow Box

• Cut along solid lines and score on dotted lines

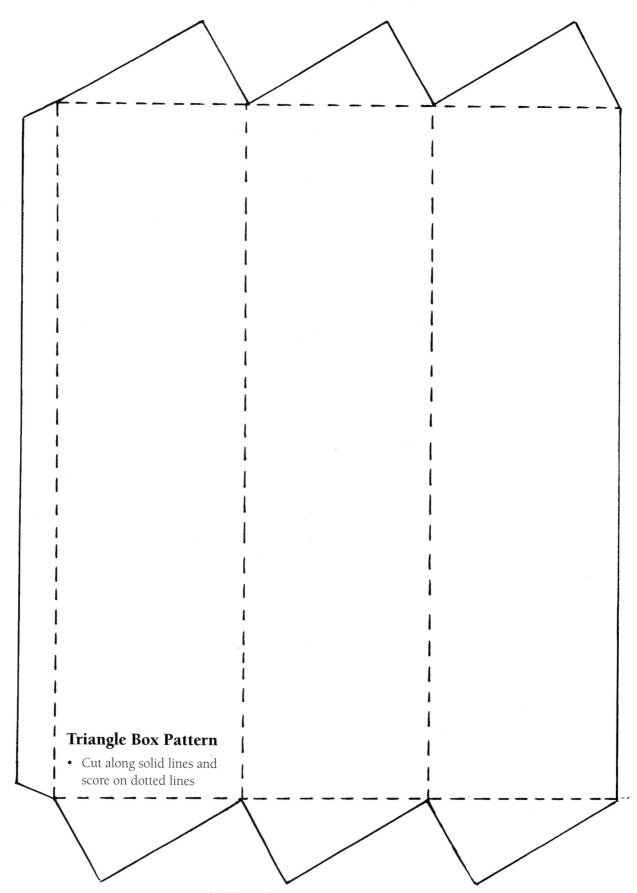

Triangle Box Pattern

- Cut along solid lines and
  score on dotted lines

How to Make Square Pinwheel Envelopes

1. Cut two strips, measuring 5" x 15", from coordinating decorative papers.

2. Score at 5" intervals as denoted in Figure 1 by the dotted lines.

3. Cut away two outer triangles on the diagonal. These are shown in Figure 1 as the shaded areas.

4. Glue the two pieces together in the center square, so they are perpendicular to one another. Figure 2 shows what the pieces look like when glued together.

5. Fold the points over, slipping the fourth point under the first point, to create a pinwheel.

6. Decorate with a 1/2" x 12" band, cut from one of the decorative papers.

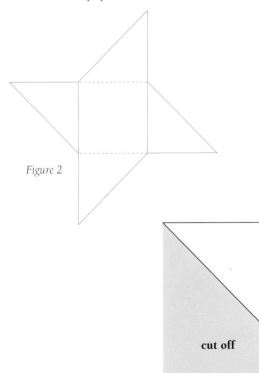

Figure 2

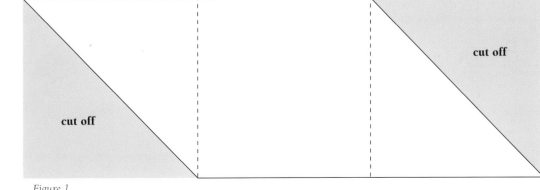

Figure 1

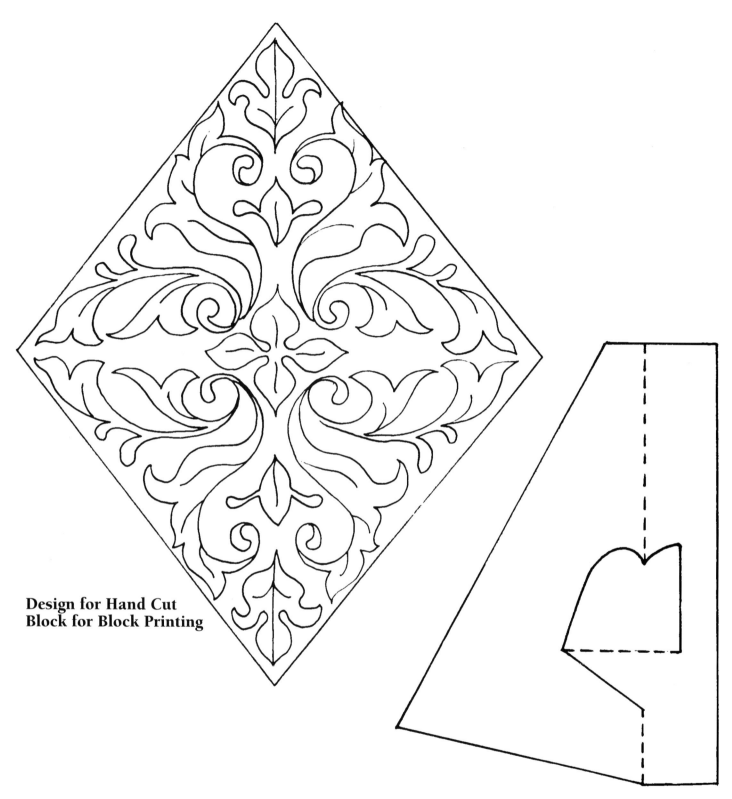

**Design for Hand Cut
Block for Block Printing**

Pattern for Frame Stand

Cut from cardboard.
Score on dotted lines. Adhere to back of matboard frames.

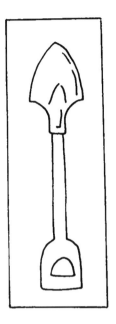

**Original Designs for
Hand Cut Blocks**

Copyright-Free Decorative Labels

Metric Conversion Chart

Inches to Millimeters and Centimeters

Inches	MM	CM	Inches	MM	CM	Inches	MM	CM
1/8	3	.3	1	25	2.5	6	152	15.2
1/4	6	.6	1-1/4	32	3.2	7	178	17.8
3/8	10	1.0	1-1/2	38	3.8	8	203	20.3
1/2	13	1.3	1-3/4	44	4.4	9	229	22.9
5/8	16	1.6	2	51	5.1	10	254	25.4
3/4	19	1.9	3	76	7.6	11	279	27.9
7/8	22	2.2	4	102	10.2	12	305	30.5
			5	127	12.7			

Yards to Meters

Yards	Meters	Yards	Meters
1/8	.11	3	2.74
1/4	.23	4	3.66
3/8	.34	5	4.57
1/2	.46	6	5.49
5/8	.57	7	6.40
3/4	.69	8	7.32
7/8	.80	9	8.23
1	.91	10	9.14
2	1.83		

Index

HILLSBORO PUBLIC LIBRARIES
Hillsboro, OR
Member of Washington County
COOPERATIVE LIBRARY SERVICES